Bohemian Grove & The Bohemian Club
The Secrecy in the Redwoods

Contents

Chapter 1

Introduction to Bohemian Grove

1.1 Bohemian Grove

Bohemian Grove is a 2,700-acre (1,100 ha) campground located at 20601 Bohemian Avenue, in Monte Rio, California, belonging to a private San Francisco-based men's art club known as the Bohemian Club. In mid-July each year, Bohemian Grove hosts a two-week, three-weekend encampment of some of the most prominent men in the world.[1][2]

1.1.1 Introduction

The Bohemian Club's all-male membership and guest list includes artists, particularly musicians, as well as many prominent business leaders, government officials (including U.S. presidents), senior media executives, and people of power.[3][4] Members may invite guests to the Grove although those guests are subject to a screening procedure. A guest's first glimpse of the Grove typically is during the "Spring Jinks" in June, preceding the main July encampment. Bohemian club members can schedule private day-use events at the Grove any time it is not being used for Club-wide purposes, and are allowed at these times to bring spouses, family and friends, though female and minor guests must be off the property by 9 or 10 pm.[5]

After 40 years of membership the men earn "Old Guard" status, giving them reserved seating at the Grove's daily talks, as well as other perquisites. Former U.S. president Herbert Hoover was inducted into the Old Guard on March 19, 1953; he had joined the club exactly 40 years prior.[6] Redwood branches from the Grove were flown to the Waldorf-Astoria Hotel in New York City where they were used to decorate a banquet room for the celebration. In his acceptance speech, Hoover compared the honor of the "Old Guard" status to his frequent role as veteran counselor to later presidents.[7]

The Club motto is "Weaving Spiders Come Not Here", which implies that outside concerns and business deals (networking) are to be left outside. When gathered in groups, Bohemians usually adhere to the injunction, though discussion of business often occurs between pairs of members.[2] Important political and business deals have been developed at the Grove.[5] The Grove is particularly famous for a Manhattan Project planning meeting that took place there in September 1942, which subsequently led to the atomic bomb. Those attending this meeting included Ernest Lawrence, U.C. Berkeley colleague Robert Oppenheimer, various military officials, the S-1 Committee heads such as the presidents of Harvard, Yale and Princeton along with representatives of Standard Oil and General Electric. At the time, Oppenheimer was not an official S-1 member due to security clearance troubles with the U.S. wartime Government, though Lawrence and Oppenheimer hosted the meeting.[8] Grove members take particular pride in this event and often relate the story to new attendees.[2]

1.1.2 History

The tradition of a summer encampment was established six years after the Bohemian Club was formed in 1872.[2] Henry "Harry" Edwards, a stage actor and founding member, announced that he was relocating to New York City to further his career. On June 29, 1878, somewhat fewer than 100 Bohemians gathered in the Redwoods in Marin County near Taylorville (present-day Samuel P. Taylor State Park) for an evening sendoff party in Edwards' honor.[9] Freely flowing liquor and some Japanese lanterns put a glow on the festivities, and club members retired at a late hour to the modest comfort of blankets laid on the dense mat of Redwood needles. This festive gathering was repeated the next year without Edwards, and became the club's yearly encampment.[10] By 1882 the members of the Club camped together at various locations in both Marin and Sonoma County, including the present-day Muir Woods and a redwood grove that once stood near Duncans Mills, several miles down the Russian River from the current location. From 1893 Bohemians rented the current location, and in 1899 purchased it from Melvin Cyrus Meeker who had developed a successful logging operation in the area.[2] Gradu-

In the 1870s, Henry "Harry" Edwards was an actor with the California Theatre Stock Company, a founding Bohemian and the head entomologist at the California Academy of Sciences

ally over the next decades, members of the Club purchased land surrounding the original location to the perimeter of the basin in which it resides.[2]

Writer and journalist William Henry Irwin said of the Grove,

> You come upon it suddenly. One step and its glory is over you. There is no perspective; you cannot get far enough away from one of the trees to see it as a whole. There they stand, a world of height above you, their pinnacles hidden by their topmost fringes of branches or lost in the sky.[11]

Not long after the Club's establishment by newspaper journalists, it was commandeered by prominent San Francisco-based businessmen, who provided the financial resources necessary to acquire further land and facilities at the Grove. However, they still retained the "bohemians"—the artists and musicians—who continued to entertain international members and guests.[2]

1.1.3 Membership and operation

The Bohemian Club is a private club; only active members of the Club and their guests may visit the Grove. These guests have been known to include politicians and notable figures from countries outside the U.S.[2] Particularly during the midsummer encampment, the number of guests is strictly limited due to the small size of the facilities.

Camp valets

Camp valets are responsible for the operation of the individual camps. The "head" valets are akin to a general manager's position at a resort, club, restaurant, or hotel. Service staff include female workers whose presence at the Grove is limited to daylight hours and to central areas close to the main gate. Male workers may be housed at the Grove within the boundaries of the camp to which they are assigned or in peripheral service areas. High-status workers stay in small private quarters but most workers are housed in rustic bunkhouses.[2]

Facilities

The main encampment area consists of 160 acres (0.65 km^2) of old-growth redwood trees over 1,000 years old, with some trees exceeding 300 feet (90 m) in height.[12]

The primary activities taking place at the Grove are varied and expansive entertainment, such as a grand main stage and a smaller, more intimate stage. Thus, the majority of common facilities are entertainment venues, interspersed among the giant redwoods.

There are also sleeping quarters, or "camps" scattered throughout the grove, of which it is reported there were a total of 118 as of 2007. These camps, which are frequently patrilineal, are the principal means through which high-level business and political contacts and friendships are formed.[2]

The pre-eminent camps are:[2][13]

- Hill Billies;
- Mandalay;
- Cave Man;
- Stowaway;
- Uplifters;
- Owls Nest;
- Hideaway;

A Typical Tent. The Occupants of This One Are Porter Garnett, George Sterling and Jack London.

A Bohemian tent in the 1900s, sheltering Porter Garnett, George Sterling and Jack London

- Isle of Aves;

- Lost Angels;

- Silverado squatters;

- Sempervirens;

- Hillside;

- Idlewild

The central spaces for recreation and entertainment are:

- *Grove Stage*—an amphitheater with seating for 2,000 used primarily for the Grove Play production, on the last weekend of the midsummer encampment. The stage extends up the hillside, and is also home to the second largest outdoor pipe organ in the world.

- *Field Circle*—a bowl-shaped amphitheater used for the mid-encampment "Low Jinks" musical comedy, for "Spring Jinks" in early June and for a variety of other performances.

- *Campfire Circle*—has a campfire pit in the middle of the circle, surrounded by carved redwood log benches.

Used for smaller performances in a more intimate setting.

- *Museum Stage*—a semi-outdoor venue with a covered stage. Lectures and small ensemble performances.

- *Dining Circle*—seating approximately 1,500 diners simultaneously.

- *Clubhouse*—designed by Bernard Maybeck in 1903, completed in 1904 on a bluff overlooking the Russian River;[14] a multi-purpose dining, drinking and entertainment building; the site of the Manhattan Project planning meeting held in 1942.

- *The Owl Shrine and the Lake*—an artificial lake in the middle of the grove, used for the noon-time concerts and also the venue of the *Cremation of Care*, which takes place on the first Saturday of the encampment. It is also the location of the 12:30 pm daily "Lakeside Talks." These significant informal talks (many on public policy issues) have been given over the years by entertainers, professors, astronauts, business leaders, cabinet officers, CIA directors, future presidents and former presidents.[15]

1.1.4 Symbolism and rituals

Since the founding of the club, the Bohemian Grove's mascot has been an owl, symbolizing knowledge. A 30-foot (9 m) hollow owl statue made of concrete over steel supports stands at the head of the lake in the Grove; this Owl Shrine was designed by sculptor and two-time club president Haig Patigian, and constructed in the late 1920s.[16][17][18][19] Since 1929, the Owl Shrine has served as the backdrop of the yearly *Cremation of Care* ceremony.[2]

The Club's patron saint is John of Nepomuk, who legend says suffered death at the hands of a Bohemian monarch rather than disclose the confessional secrets of the queen. A large wood carving of St. John in cleric robes with his index finger over his lips stands at the shore of the lake in the Grove, symbolizing the secrecy kept by the Grove's attendees throughout its long history.[2]

Cremation of Care

The *Cremation of Care* ceremony was first conducted in the Bohemian Grove at the Midsummer encampment in 1881, devised by James F. Bowman with George T. Bromley playing the High Priest.[20] It was originally set up within the plot of the serious "High Jinks" dramatic performance on the first weekend of the summer encampment, after which the spirit of "Care", slain by the Jinks hero, was solemnly cremated. The ceremony served as a catharsis for pent-up

THE CREMATION OF CARE (1907)

Cremation of Care *in 1907*

A SCENE FROM "ST. PATRICK AT TARA"
FROM A PHOTOGRAPH TAKEN IN DAYTIME DURING THE DRESS REHEARSAL
PHOTOGRAPH BY GABRIEL MOULIN

A dress rehearsal for the 1909 Grove Play, St. Patrick at Tara

high spirits, and "to present symbolically the salvation of the trees by the club ..."[21] The *Cremation of Care* was separated from the Grove Play in 1913 and moved to the first night to become "an exorcising of the Demon to ensure the success of the ensuing two weeks."[22] The Grove Play was moved to the last weekend of the encampment.[23]

The ceremony takes place in front of the Owl Shrine, a 30-foot (9 m) hollow owl statue made of concrete over steel supports. The moss- and lichen-covered statue simulates a natural rock formation, yet holds electrical and audio equipment within it. For many years, a recording of the voice of club member Walter Cronkite was used as the voice of The Owl during the ceremony.[1] Music and pyrotechnics accompany the ritual for dramatic effect.

Grove Play

Main article: List of Grove Plays

Each year, a Grove Play is performed for one night during the final weekend of the summer encampment. The play

is a large-scale musical theatrical production, written and composed by club members, involving some 300 people, including chorus, cast, stage crew and orchestra.[24] The first Grove Play was performed in 1902; during the war years 1943–1945 the stage was dark. In 1975, an observer estimated that the Grove Play cost between $20,000 and $30,000, an amount that would be as high as $131,000 in today's dollars.[24]

1.1.5   Criticism and controversy

With its combination of wealth and power, Bohemian Grove's secrecy has been a target for protest for many years. The Bohemian Grove Action Network of Occidental, California, organizes protests and has aided journalists who wish to penetrate the secrecy surrounding the encampment. Over the years, individuals have infiltrated the Grove then later published video and claimed accounts of the activities at Bohemian Grove.

Infiltrations

In the summer of 1989, *Spy* magazine writer Philip Weiss spent some seven days in the camp posing as a guest, which led to his November 1989 article "Inside Bohemian Grove".[1] He wrote about uninhibited behavior he witnessed: "You know you are inside the Bohemian Grove when you come down a trail in the woods and hear piano music from amid a group of tents and then round a bend to see a man with a beer in one hand and his penis in the other, urinating into the bushes. This is the most gloried-in ritual of the encampment, the freedom of powerful men to pee wherever they like ..."[1] Weiss noticed "hundreds of cigars whose smokers had ignited them in defiance of the California Forest Service's posted warnings."[1]

On July 15, 2000, controversial conspiracy theorist Alex Jones and his cameraman, Mike Hanson, snuck into the Grove. Jones' investigation was discussed by Jon Ronson in Channel 4's five-part documentary, *Secret Rulers of the World*. Ronson documented his view of the ritual in his book, *Them: Adventures With Extremists*, writing "My lasting impression was of an all-pervading sense of immaturity: the Elvis impersonators, the pseudo-pagan spooky rituals, the heavy drinking. These people might have reached the apex of their professions but emotionally they seemed trapped in their college years."[25]

On January 19, 2002, 37-year-old Richard McCaslin was arrested after his nighttime infiltration of the Bohemian Grove, where he set several fires. He was heavily armed and wearing a skull mask and outfit with "Phantom Patriot" written across the chest.[26]

The Owl Shrine covered in moss, standing among trees behind a stage at one edge of a man-made pond

Women

Though no woman has ever been given full membership in the Bohemian Club, the four female honorary members were hostess Margaret Bowman, poet Ina Coolbrith (who served as librarian for the Club), actress Elizabeth Crocker Bowers and writer Sara Jane Lippincott.[23] Since Coolbrith's death in 1928, no other woman has been made a member. These honorary members and other women guests have been allowed into the Bohemian "City Club" building and as daytime guests of the Grove, but not to the upper floors of the City Club nor as guests to the main summer encampment at the Grove.[23] Annual "Ladies' Jinks" were held at the Club especially for spouses and invited guests.[23]

In 1978 the Bohemian Club was charged with discrimination by the California Department of Fair Employment and Housing over its refusal to hire women employees. In January 1981, an administrative law judge issued a decision supporting the practices of the Club, noting that club members at the Grove "urinate in the open without even the use of rudimentary toilet facilities" and that the presence of females would alter club members' behavior.[27] However, the judge's decision was overruled by the State Fair Employment and Housing Commission, which on October 17, 1981, ordered the Club to begin recruiting and hiring women as employees.[28] In 1986 the Bohemian Club went to the California Supreme Court over the issue, arguing that their freedom of association was being harmed; the Court found against the Club and denied a review in 1987, forcing the Club to begin hiring female workers during the summer encampment at the Grove in Monte Rio.[29] This ruling became quoted as a legal precedent and was discussed during the 1995–1996 floor debate surrounding California Senate Bill SB 2110 (Maddy), a proposed bill concerning whether tax-exempt organizations (including fraternal clubs) should be exempt from the Unruh Civil Rights Act.[30]

Logging

Outside the central camp area which is the site of the old-growth grove, but within the 2,712 acres (10.98 km^2) owned by the Bohemian Club, logging activities have been underway since 1984. Approximately 11,000,000 board feet (26,000 m^3) of lumber equivalents were removed from the surrounding redwood and Douglas fir forest from 1984 to 2007. In 2007, the Bohemian Club board filed application for a nonindustrial logging permit available to landowners with less than 2,500 acres (10 km^2) of timberland, which would allow them to steadily increase their logging in the second-growth stands from 800,000 board feet (1,900 m^3) per year to 1,700,000 board feet (4,000 m^3) over the course of the 50-year permit.[31] The board had been advised by Tom Bonnicksen, a retired forestry professor, that they should conduct group selection logging to reduce the risk of fire burning through the dense second-growth stands, damaging the old-growth forest the Club wants to protect. The Bohemian Club stated that an expansion of logging activities was needed to prevent fires, and that money made from the sale of the lumber would be used to stabilize access roads and to clear fire-promoting species like tanoaks and underbrush.[32] The California Department of Fish and Game, have instead recommended single-tree logging to preserve the habitats of murrelets and spotted owls in senescent trees. Philip Rundel, University of California, Berkeley professor of biology said that redwoods are not very flammable and "This is clearly a logging project, not a project to reduce fire hazard".[31] Reed F. Noss, professor at the University of California, Davis, has written that fires within redwood forests do not need to be prevented, that young redwoods are adapted to regenerate well in the destruction left behind by the fires typical of the climate.[33]

After controversy raised by opponents of the harvesting plan, the club moved to clearly establish their qualification for the permit by offering 163 acres (0.66 km^2) to the Rocky Mountain Elk Foundation in Missoula, Montana for a conservation easement. A further 56.75 acres (229,700 m^2) were written off as not being available for commercial logging, bringing the total to 2,316 acres (9.37 km^2) and thereby qualifying for the permit. Opponents and their lawyers interpret the relevant law as counting all timberland and not just that actually subject to the logging permit. They state that if the total of timberland is counted, 2,535.75 acres (10.2618 km^2) are owned by the club, so the permit should not be granted.[31]

On March 10, 2011, Judge René A. Chouteau rejected the Non-Industrial Timber Management Plan (NTMP) that Cal-Fire had approved. The suit, brought by the Sierra Club and the Bohemian Redwood Rescue Club, sought to have the NTMP annulled. The ruling calls on the Bohemian Club to draft a new NTMP that offers alternatives to its proposed rate of logging. At present the Bohemian Club is not allowed to log any of its property.[34]

1.1.6 Fictional depictions

A large portion of the novel *Significant Others* by Armistead Maupin takes place in the Bohemian Grove, where the rituals are described in detail.

Harry Shearer's movie *Teddy Bears' Picnic* is about an annual encampment of prominent male leaders at the Zambezi Glen, a thinly-veiled reference to the Bohemian Grove. Shearer attended at least one Bohemian event.[35]

1.1.7 See also

- Belizean Grove
- List of Bohemian Club members
- The Family (club)
- Rancheros visitadores

1.1.8 References

Notes

[1] Philip Weiss. "Masters of the Universe Go to Camp: Inside the Bohemian Grove". *Spy Magazine*. November 1989.

[2] "Peter Martin Phillips, A Relative Advantage: Sociology of the San Francisco Bohemian Club], 1994.". Retrieved 14 July 2014.

[3] Wallace Turner. "At the Bohemian Club, men join, women serve", *The New York Times*, January 12, 1981

[4] Inside Bohemian Grove from Fairness & Accuracy In Reporting Nov–Dec 1991

[5] Nick Schou (August 31, 2006). "Bohemian Grove Exposes Itself!". OC Weekly.

[6] Van der Zee, John (1974). *The Greatest Men's Party on Earth: Inside the Bohemian Grove*. Harcourt Brace Javonovich. p. 88. ISBN 0-15-136905-4.

[7] Wert, Hal Elliott (2005). *Hoover, the Fishing President: Portrait of the Private Man and His Life Outdoors*. Stackpole Books. p. 309. ISBN 0-8117-0099-2.

[8] Brotherhood of the Bomb by Gregg Herken Chapter 4

[9] Garnett, 1908, p. 6.

[10] Garnett, 1908, p. 7.

[11] Garnett, 1908, p. 8.

[12] Jane Kay (July 12, 2007). "Bohemian Club's logging plan raises plenty of sawdust". *SF Gate*. Retrieved September 16, 2008.

[13] Louis E. Gelwicks. *The Camps: Facts, Artifacts and Fantasies* 1979

[14] Vernacular Language North. Bernard Maybeck. *Bohemian Clubhouse*. Retrieved March 4, 2009.

[15] Domhoff, G. William, *The Bohemian Grove and Other Retreats: A study in ruling class cohesiveness*, Harper and Row, 1974.

[16] Jewell, James E. (1997). *The Visual Arts in Bohemia: 125 years of artistic creativity in the Bohemian Club*. Annals of the Bohemian Club **8**. Bohemian Club. pp. 135, 326.

[17] Graves, Gary John (1993). *The Bohemian Grove Theatrics: A History and Analysis from the Club's Beginnings in 1872 up to the Encampment of 1992*. University of California, Berkeley. p. 7.

[18] Pugh, Simon (1988). *Garden, Nature, Language*. Manchester University Press. p. 43. ISBN 9780719028250. Quoting *The Guardian*, London, November 24, 1986.

[19] Starr, Kevin (2002). *The Dream Endures: California Enters the 1940s*. Oxford University Press. ISBN 0-19-515797-4.

[20] Garnett, 1908, p. 19.

[21] Garnett, 1908, p. 25.

[22] Ogden, Dunbar H.; Douglas McDermott; Robert Károly Sarlós (1990). *Theatre West: Image and Impact*. Rodopi. p. 36. ISBN 90-5183-125-0.

[23] Ogden, 1990, p. 36.

[24] Domhoff, 1975, p. 10

[25] Ronson, Jon (2002). *Them: Adventures with Extremists*. Simon and Schuster. p. 321. ISBN 0-7432-3321-2. Retrieved April 18, 2010.

[26] Masked man enters, attacks Bohemian Grove:'Phantom' expected armed resistance, by Peter Fimrite, *San Francisco Chronicle*, January 24, 2002

[27] "Bohemian Club Is Upheld On Refusal to Hire Women". NYTimes.com. January 23, 1981.

[28] Katherine Bishop (October 17, 1981). "Bohemian Club Ordered To Begin Hiring Women". NYTimes.com.

[29] "RETREAT MAY BE CLUB'S LAST WITHOUT WOMEN". July 8, 1987.

[30] California State Senate. 1995–1996 Senate Bills. *SB 2110*

[31] Kay, Jane (July 6, 2009). "No retreat from uproar over Bohemian Club woods". *San Francisco Chronicle*. Retrieved July 14, 2009.

[32] Henley, Patricia Lynn. *Metroactive*, July 4–10, 2007. "Timber! Bohemian Club's long-term logging plan draws fire." Retrieved October 1, 2009.

[33] Noss, Reed F.; Save-the-Redwoods League. *The redwood forest: history, ecology, and conservation of the coast redwoods*, p. 231. Island Press, 2000. ISBN 1-55963-726-9

[34] Zito, Kelly (March 15, 2011). "Bohemian Club's 100-year logging permit revoked". *San Francisco Chronicle*. Retrieved March 22, 2011.

[35] New York Times. Movie Review. Dave Kehr. March 29, 2002. *Teddy Bear's Picnic (2002)*

Bibliography

- Domhoff, G. William. *The Bohemian Grove and Other Retreats: A study in ruling class cohesiveness*, Harper and Row, 1974.

- Field, Charles K. *The Cremation of Care*, 1946, 1953

- Fletcher, Robert H. *The Annals of the Bohemian Club*, Hicks-Judd, 1900

- Garnett, Porter. *The Bohemian Jinks: A Treatise*, 1908

- Hanson, Mike. *Bohemian Grove: Cult Of Conspiracy*, iUniverse Inc, 2004

- Hodapp, Christopher; Alice Von Kannon (2008). *Conspiracy Theories & Secret Societies For Dummies*. Hoboken, NJ: Wiley. ISBN 0-470-18408-6.

- Hoover, Herbert. *Memoirs, Vol 2: The Cabinet and the Presidency*, Macmillan, 1952.

  - Hoover was a prominent figure in the Grove's history and coined the phrase: "*The Greatest Men's Party on Earth*".

- Hotaling, Richard M; Sabin, Wallace Arthur; and Sterling, George. "Bohemian Grove" in *The Twilight of Kings: A Masque of Democracy*, the 16th Grove play (1918)

- Ickes, Harold L.. *The Secret Diary of Harold L. Ickes, Vol 1. The First Thousand Days, 1933–36*. Simon and Schuster, 1953.

  - Ickes was Secretary of the Interior during the New Deal.

- Isaacson, Walter. *Kissinger: A Biography*, New York: Simon & Schuster, 1992, (updated) 2005.

  - Contains a brief reference to his attendance at the Grove and fame for his performances in various skits.

- Maupin, Armistead. *Significant Others*, Chatto and Windus, 1988.

  - A fictionalized account of the grove, as described from the point of view of one of the major characters in the fifth of the *Tales of the City* series. Sympathetic and well informed, it includes an accurate description of the *Cremation of Care* ceremony.

- McCartney, Laton. *Friends in High Places: The Bechtel Story: The Most Secret Corporation and how It Engineered the World*, Ballantine Books, Updated edition, 1989.

  - For the network of links between the Californian-based and privately owned Bechtel Corporation and members of Reagan's Cabinet, along with their camp membership in the Grove.

- Nader, Ralph. *The Big Boys*, Pantheon, 1987.

  - Contains a chapter on high-level businessmen and the tightly held secrecy of their Club membership.

- Nixon, Richard. *RN : The Memoirs of Richard Nixon*, Grosset & Dunlap, 1978.

- Phillips, Peter Martin. *A Relative Advantage: Sociology of the San Francisco Bohemian Club*

  - A definitive look at the history of the Grove and the composition of Bohemian Club members and their social, business and political affiliations, updating Domhoff's book (see above). Phillips is Professor of Sociology at Sonoma State University in California. He attended events at the Grove and conducted scores of interviews with attendees in his research.

- Quigley, Carroll. *Tragedy And Hope: A History of the World in Our Time*, G. S. G. & Associates, Incorporated, 1975.

  - This book serves as the basis for many current conspiracy theories and studies of socioeconomic elites.

- Schmidt, Helmut, *Men and Powers : A Political Retrospective*, Random House, 1990.

  - Schmidt states that Germany had similar institutions, some of which included such rituals as *Cremation of Care*, but that his favorite was the Bohemian Grove.

- Shultz, George P.. *Turmoil and Triumph: Diplomacy, Power and the Victory of the American Ideal*, Macmillan Publishing Company, 1993.

- Stephens, Henry Morse; Sabin, Wallace Arthur; and Dobie, Charles Caldwell. "Bohemian Club" in *St. Patrick at Tara*, 1909 Grove play

- Warren, Earl. *The Memoirs of Chief Justice Earl Warren*, Madison Books, 2001. A frequent attendee, Warren mentions the Grove in his reminiscences.

- Watson, Thomas J. Jr. and Petre, Peter. *Father, Son & Co. : My Life at IBM and Beyond*, Bantam, 2000. An IBM CEO gives an insider's business perspective on the Grove.

1.1.9   External links

- "An Elite Alliance". March 2006, article on former NASA head and current LSU Chancellor Sean O'Keefe's participation in the Bohemian Grove.

- Images of Bohemian Grove, ca. 1906–1909, The Bancroft Library.

- "Old Bohemia, New Bohemia" (compares Bohemian Grove and Burning Man). *Forbes Magazine*. 1999.

- William F. Buckley, Jr. "Newt Draws Fire". *National Review*. September 11, 1995. *On The Right*. Rebuts stories of men running around naked at the Grove.

- Save Bohemian Grove The website of the group that brought suit against the Grove for its logging practices.

- "The Bohemian Club Grove Play". UNZ.org.

- "The Phoenix Nest". UNZ.org.

- Richard Nixon 1967 speech at the Bohemian Groove Nixon Foundation

1.2   Henry Edwards (entomologist)

This article is about the England-born actor and entomologist. For the American entomologist, see William Henry Edwards.

Henry Edwards (August 27, 1827 – June 9, 1891), known as "**Harry**", was an English-born stage actor, writer and entomologist who gained fame in Australia, San Francisco and New York City for his theater work.

Edwards was drawn to the theater early in life, and he appeared in amateur productions in London. After sailing to Australia, Edwards appeared professionally in Shakespearean plays and light comedies primarily in Melbourne and Sydney. Throughout his childhood in England and his acting career in Australia, he was greatly interested in collecting insects, and the National Museum of Victoria used the results of his Australian fieldwork as part of the genesis of their collection.

In San Francisco, Edwards was a founding member of the Bohemian Club, and a gathering in Edwards' honor was the spark which began the club's traditional summer encampment at the Bohemian Grove.[3] As well, Edwards cemented his reputation as a preeminent stage actor and theater manager. After writing a series of influential studies on Pacific Coast butterflies and moths he was elected life member of the California Academy of Sciences. Relocating to the East Coast, Edwards spent a brief time in Boston theater. This led to a connection to Wallack's Theatre and further renown in New York City. There, Edwards edited three volumes of the journal *Papilio* and published a major work about the life of the butterfly.[2] His large collection of insect specimens served as the foundation of the American Museum of Natural History's butterfly and moth studies.

Edwards' wide-ranging studies and observations of insects brought him into contact with specimens not yet classified. Upon discovering previously unknown insects he would give them names, which led to a number of butterfly, moth and beetle species bearing "Hy. Edw." (for Henry Edwards) as an attribution.[4] From his theater interests to entomology, Edwards carried forward an appreciation of Shakespeare—in the designation of new insect species he favored female character names from Shakespeare's plays.

1.2.1   Early career

Henry Edwards was born to Hannah and Thomas Edwards (c. 1794 – 1857) at Brook House in Ross-on-Wye, Herefordshire, England, on August 27, 1827, and was christened on September 14.[5] From his older brother William, he picked up an interest in examining insects. He collected butterflies as a hobby, and studied them under the tutelage of Edward Doubleday. His solicitor father intended a law career for his son, but after a brief period of unsuccessful study, Edwards took a position at a counting house in London, and began acting in amateur theater. He then journeyed to join his brother William who had settled in Australia, nine miles (14 km) north-west of Melbourne along the bank of Merri Creek, a location then called Merrivale. Aboard the sailing ship *Ganges* from March to June 1853, he wrote descriptions of creatures such as the albatross that he encountered for the first time.[5] After arriving in Melbourne, Edwards began collecting and cataloging the insects he found on his brother's land, and further afield. Within two years, he had gathered 1,676 species of insects, shot and mounted 200 birds, and pressed some 200 botanical specimens.[5] This collection and that of William Kershaw were purchased by Frederick McCoy to form the nucleus of the new National Museum of Victoria.[5]

The first Australian stage appearance by Edwards was with George Selth Coppin's company at the Queen's Theatre in Melbourne. Later, he joined Gustavus Vaughan Brooke's theatrical group. The part of Petruchio, the male lead in Shakespeare's *The Taming of the Shrew*, was filled by Edwards at the Princess's Theatre in Sydney in November, 1859, playing opposite tragedian Avonia Jones as Katharine.[6] In December that year Brooke retired from management, yielding the reins of his company to the team of Edwards and George Fawcett Rowe, English actor and playwright. Brooke continued to act under Edwards and Rowe: his starring performance in April 1860 as Louis XI in Dion Boucicault's play of the same name was a stirring portrayal that Edwards, playing Jacques d'Armagnac, Duke of Nemours, recalled vividly for the rest of his life.[6] Sharing the stage again in August, Brooke and Edwards were well received in their portrayal of twin brothers in a production of Shakespeare's *The Comedy of Errors* in Melbourne, the first Australian mounting of that work.[6] As a twist to pique public interest, Edwards and Brooke exchanged roles after two weeks' run. However, not all of Edwards' performances were successful: his turn at Angelo in Shakespeare's *Measure for Measure* was called "invertebrate"[6] by drama critic William John Lawrence; in Lawrence's estimation, Edwards and his fellow actors paled against the powerful performance of Avonia Jones as Isabella.[6]

The renowned entomologist and collector William Sharp Macleay was sought out by Edwards whenever his stage appearances took him to Sydney. Beginning in 1858, Macleay mentored Edwards and encouraged him to search for more insect specimens when his theater obligations allowed. Robust and adventuresome, Edwards occasionally trekked out into the wilds of Australia on the hunt for insects. While in Sydney, Edwards went up two times in a hot air balloon as a favor to George Coppin, narrowly avoiding severe injury or death in the first ascent.[7] Edwards' further travels included New Zealand,[8] Peru, Panama and Mexico in pursuit of insects and dramatic roles.[4]

1.2.2 San Francisco

In 1865, Edwards began a 12-year residence in San Francisco, California. At the 1870 United States Census, Edwards reported himself as a non-voting foreign-born resident, a comedian by trade, living in a home worth $1,000.[9] Edwards lived in San Francisco with a white woman listed in the census as "Mariana", born in England, age 40, and

a 16-year-old Chinese servant named Heng Gim.[9] The woman Mariana was likely Edwards's wife,[10] the former Marianne Elizabeth Woolcott Bray who was born about 1822–1823 in New Street, Birmingham.[6] In 1851 at the age of 28, Bray married Gustavus Vaughan Brooke, and the two went to Australia to manage Brooke's then-new theater company. It was there that Edwards met Brooke and his wife, but after several years of the two men working together, Brooke remarried in February 1863, taking Avonia Jones (1836–1867)[11] as his second wife. Brooke died in an accident at sea in January 1866, and Avonia Jones Brooke died in New York City the next year.[12] Later reports spoke of Edwards marrying Brooke's widow, without naming her.[10]

Theatre card

In 1868–1869 Edwards leased and managed the Metropolitan Theater,[13] and he was a founding member of the acting company of the California Theatre, which opened in January 1869.[14] The theater was directed and managed by actor John McCullough, and among the more notable productions was *As You Like It* in May 1872, with McCullough playing Orlando and Edwards the banished Duke Senior. Walter M. Leman, who carried the part of Adam, opined in 1886 that "never since *time was* has Shakespeare's charming idyl been better put upon the stage."[15]

Edwards was one of the founders and the first vice president of the Bohemian Club, and served two terms as president, 1873–1875.[16] He hosted Shakespeare celebrations at the club in April 1873, 1875 and 1877, and a Bohemian Christmas celebration in December 1877: "The Feast of Reason and Flow of Soul".[17] Edwards became a director of the San Francisco Art Association, and spoke for Lotta Crabtree at the dedication of Lotta's Fountain in September, 1875.[13]

Still very much interested in insects, Edwards spent his spare time at the California Academy of Sciences studying butterflies under Hans Hermann Behr, the academy's curator for Lepidoptera, the scientific order of moths and butterflies.[4] Elected a member of the academy in 1867, he concentrated on describing the structure and habits of moths and butterflies on the Pacific coast from British Columbia to Baja California. He went to visit John Muir in Yosemite Valley in June 1871, with a letter of introduction from Jeanne Carr, the wife of California's chief geologist Ezra S. Carr. The letter described Edwards as "one of Nature's truest and most devoted disciples", a sojourner who "has the keys to the Kingdom".[18] After the visit, Muir occasionally sent specimens from the Sierras to add to Edwards' collection, carried to San Francisco by men such as geologist and artist Clarence King who were returning from Yosemite field study. Edwards presented a series of papers to the academy entitled *Pacific Coast Lepidoptera*,[13] and classified two species as new to science. He named one *Gyros muiri* for Muir, with "Hy. Edw." as the attribution.[19] In 1872, Muir sent Edwards a letter, writing "You are now in constant remembrance, because every flying flower is branded with your name."[4] In 1873, Edwards became the curator of entomology at the academy, and began to serve on the Publications Committee which produced the journal *Proceedings of the California Academy of Sciences*. Beginning early that year, he accompanied and befriended George Robert Crotch on the latter's insect-collecting tour of California, Oregon and British Columbia. In 1874, Edwards began to serve as one of the academy's vice presidents, and for the academy in late 1874 after Crotch's death from tuberculosis, he published a memorial tribute to the man.[20] Edwards also wrote one of many tributes to academician Louis Agassiz at his death in late 1873. At the academy on January 2, 1877, Edwards was elected member for life.[21]

Though successful in San Francisco, Edwards decided to head for Boston and New York City to see if his career as an actor could benefit from appearances in the eastern United States.[22] On June 29, 1878, somewhat fewer than 100 of his Bohemian friends gathered in the woods near Taylorville, California (present-day Samuel P. Taylor State Park), for a night-time send-off party in Edwards' honor.[23] Bohemian Club historian Porter Garnett later wrote that the men at the "nocturnal picnic" were "provided with blankets to keep them warm and a generous supply of liquor for the same purpose".[3] Japanese lanterns were used for illumination and decoration. This festive gathering was repeated without Edwards by club members the next year, and every year thereafter, eventually evolving and expanding into the club's annual summer encampment at the Bohemian Grove,[3] famous (or infamous) for the casual commingling of top politicians and powerful captains of industry in attendance.[24]

1.2.3   Boston to New York

In late 1878, Edwards joined a theater company in Boston, replacing another actor as "Schelm, Chief of Police" at a revival of the spectacle *The Exiles* at the Boston Theatre on Washington Street.[25] After a four-week run, he performed in other productions at the theater through the 1879–1880 season.[26] In June, Edwards answered the 1880 census to report himself an England-born actor living with his English wife "Marian" and his Chinese servant, Gim Hing.[27]

Edwards in New York

From Boston, Edwards moved to New York to stay for some ten years, performing on stage and participating in insect studies. He was active in the Brooklyn and New York Entomological Societies. In 1881, he co-founded and edited a butterfly enthusiast's periodical entitled *Papilio*, named for the genus *Papilio* in the swallowtail butterfly family, Papilionidae.[4] Edwards served as editor until January 1884 when he gave the reins to his friend Eugene Murray-Aaron of Philadelphia.[28] *Papilio* was published until 1885 when its subscription base was merged into the more general *Entomologia Americana*, published by the Brooklyn Entomological Society.

Beginning in December 1880 under Lester Wallack, the charismatic son of the theater's founder, Edwards was associated with Wallack's Theatre in New York, called the "finest theatre company in America".[29] Now in his 50s, the entomologist and actor appeared in such representative British dramatic roles as Prince Malleotti in *Forget Me Not*, Max Harkaway in *London Assurance*, Baron Stein in *Diplomacy*, and Master Walter in *The Hunchback*, reprising James Sheridan Knowles's earlier portrayal. Edwards used Wallack's Theatre as his professional mailing address, and helped manage it upon occasion. Wallack, already head "Shepherd" of the Lambs Club, a modest meetinghouse of professional stage actors, invited Edwards to join.[30] Once a Lamb, Edwards threw his energies in with those of Wallack and other club members to aid newspaper editor Harrison Grey Fiske in the organization of a charitable fund to support destitute actors or their widows. Wallack was made president of the resulting Actors' Fund. A year after its first meeting on July 15, 1882 at Wallack's Theatre, Edwards was made secretary, a position he held for one year. His wife joined the Women's Executive Committee of the Fund.[31]

Edwards appeared in early 1882 at Palmer's Theatre on Broadway and West 30th Street in a production of the English comedy *The School for Scandal*. Wallack stalwart John Gibbs Gilbert reached the height of his fame in the production, playing Sir Peter Teazle. As Sir Oliver Surface, Edwards, too, was lauded—Gilbert and Edwards shared the stage with Stella Boniface, Osmond Tearle, Gerald Eyre, Madame Ponisi and Rose Coghlan.[32]

Gathering together under one cover his various short subjects, essays, and elegies to fallen friends, Edwards published in 1883 a wryly humorous book entitled *A Mingled Yarn*, including tales of travels and stories of his time in the Bohemian Club. Dedicated to the Bohemians, "with grateful memories, and feelings of affectionate regard,"[33] the book was favorably reviewed in the *New York Tribune*. This review was reprinted in the *Literary News*: "Mr. Edwards—remarkable for attainments in science no less than for versatile proficiency in the art of acting—presents a rare type of the union of talents greatly divergent and seldom found in one and the same person."[34]

In 1886, Edwards was interviewed for *The Theatre*, a weekly magazine published in New York. Edwards was described as "unusually popular and genial", with a "charming English" wife and a Chinese servant named Charlie who "adores his employers" and had served them for 17 years.[35] The Edwards' home was observed to be comfortable but decorated with an astonishing collection of wonders from around the globe. Displayed amid the biological specimens, rugs, china, furniture, and valuable photographs were paintings executed by other actors, including ones by Edward Askew Sothern and Joseph Jefferson.

"Harry" Edwards was interviewed by The Theatre *magazine in 1886.*

Edwards showed letters he had received from a wide array of notables such as writers William Makepeace Thackeray, Charles Dickens, Anthony Trollope and naturalists Charles Darwin, Louis Agassiz and John Lubbock, 1st Baron Avebury. One floor of the residence was seen to be wholly devoted to the entomologist's collection of specimens, which Edwards said was insured for $17,000,[35] $446,000 in current value. Surrounded by his exotic possessions and "in the most perfect congeniality with his wife", Edwards was reported to be the host of a "cultivated home".[35]

1.2.4 Last years

Two years after Alfred, Lord Tennyson, completed his *Idylls of the King*, a poetic telling of the King Arthur legend, Edwards and George Parsons Lathrop adapted it to the stage as a drama in four acts. The result was *Elaine*, a story of young love between Elaine of Astolat and Lancelot, fashioned with "flower-like fragility" and "winning touches of tenderness".[36] Its first public presentation was a staged "author's reading" at Madison Square Theatre on April 28, 1887, at which Edwards played the part of Elaine's father, Lord Astolat.[37] Months later it was presented by the company of A. M. Palmer, without Edwards in the cast, opening on December 6, 1887, at the same venue. The production proved both popular and profitable for Lathrop and Edwards.[38] Annie Russell's Elaine was admired for her "sweet simplicity and pathos which captured nearly every heart".[39] After a successful six-week New York run, Palmer took *Elaine* on the road.[36][38]

Actors associated with Wallack's Theatre announced to the public that beginning in February 1888 a final series of old comedies would be revived, after which the company would be disbanded.[36] Edwards served as stage manager for the run, and reprised several of his earlier roles including those of Max Harkaway in *London Assurance* and Colonel Rockett in *Old Heads and Young Hearts*.[40] Taking part once again in *The School for Scandal*, the sixth and final play of the nostalgic series, Edwards received high praise for his depiction of a wealthy Englishman recently returned from India: "there is probably no better Sir Oliver on our stage than Mr. Edwards."[36] "Justly esteemed"[10] in the role, he was called a "sterling player", representative "of a school which is fast disappearing".[36]

A testimonial production of *Hamlet* was mounted at the Metropolitan Opera House on May 21, 1888, to celebrate the life and accomplishments of an aging Lester Wallack, and to raise money to ease the chronic sciatica that arrested his career. "One of the greatest casts ever assembled"[29] was formed into a company composed of Edwards as the priest, Edwin Booth as Hamlet, Lawrence Barrett as the ghost, Frank Mayo as the king, John Gibbs Gilbert as Polonius, Rose Coghlan as the player queen and Helena Modjeska as Ophelia. Other stars made cameo appearances, and Wallack was assisted up onto the stage to address the standing room crowd at intermission. Notables such as Mayor Hewitt and General Sherman were in attendance. More than $10,000 was raised for Wallack's care. In the following months, Edwards teamed with other actors and Wallack's wife to help him write his memoir;[41] Wallack died in September.[29]

The next year, Edwards published a significant treatise entitled *Bibliographic Catalogue of the Described Transformation of North American Lepidoptera*.[4] In response to an invitation and after arranging a business contract, he traveled back to Australia to accept a position as stage manager of a theatrical company in Melbourne. Frustrated with the experience, Edwards sailed back to New York the next year with the intention of returning to acting, but poor health kept him from full enjoyment of the limelight. In March, Edwards appeared as Holofernes in *Love's Labour's Lost* at Augustin Daly's Daly Theatre, but was often short of breath and unable to keep pace with the run—his part was given to a young Tyrone Power who also covered Edwards' old role of Sir Oliver Surface for Daly's road show of *The School for Scandal*.[10]

To regain his strength, Edwards and his wife took a carriage to a rustic cottage refuge in Arkville in the Catskill Mountains but isolation, plain food and rest yielded little improvement. A physician was called and he informed Mrs. Edwards that there would be no recovery for her husband from the advanced Bright's disease with complications from chronic pneumonia[10] so she brought him back to New York City. Edwards died at home at 185 East 116th Street in East Harlem late on June 9, 1891, just hours after returning.[4]

1.2.5 Legacy

After his death, Edwards' collection of 300,000 insect specimens,[2] one of the largest in the United States, was bought by his friends for $15,000[42] for the financial benefit of his widow, and donated to the American Museum of Natural History (AMNH) as the cornerstone of their collection.[4] Mrs. Harry Edwards also donated some of his other specimens, including two eggs of the order Rajiformes, the true rays.[43] Museum trustees purchased the 500 volumes of entomology texts and 1,200 pamphlets[44] owned by Edwards to form the "Harry Edwards Entomological Library", one of the handful of important book acquisitions made by the AMNH to expand their library in its early years.[45] William Schaus, a student that Edwards guided and encouraged, but never met in person,[5] went on to further define moth and butterfly characteristics in a large body of published work.[4]

The "Hy. Edw." designation appended to some butterfly species names indicates first description by Henry Edwards. This is not to be confused with the "Edw." designation which stands for William Henry Edwards, an unrelated contemporary and correspondent of Edwards'.[4] At least two specimens were designated "Mrs. Hy. Edwards." because they were collected and identified by his wife.[46][47] Edwards named many butterflies in the families Theclinae, Nymphalidae, Papilionidae and Lycaenidae, but his largest contribution was in the description of moth species in North America including Mexico: Arctiidae, Bombycidae, Hepialidae, Sesiidae, Noctuidae, Sphingidae, Lasiocampidae, Dalceridae, Dysderidae, Geometridae, Pyralidae, Saturniidae, Thyatiridae, Urodidae and Zygaenidae.[8] In choosing names, Edwards favored female characters from the plays of William Shakespeare, such as Ophelia from *Hamlet*, Hermia from *A Midsummer Night's Dream*, and Desdemona from *Othello*.[48] For example, Edwards collected, classified and named the moth species *Catocala ophelia*[49] and *Catocala hermia* in 1880,[50] and *Catocala desdemona* in 1882.[51]

Birth dates

The birth date that Edwards gave as his own varied depending on the time and place he was asked. Parish records show he was christened in England on September 14, 1827, and corroborating this date he gave his age as 25 in June 1853 when he first arrived in Australia.[5] However, when questioned in San Francisco for the 1870 United States Census, he gave his birth year as 1830.[9] Ten years later in Boston, he reported his age as 45,[9] implying a birth year of 1835, but he returned to supplying the year 1830 along with the date August 27 for the brief biographical sketches used by theater and entomological publications. Two years before he died, he told a reporter from the *Lorgnette* that he was born in 1832.[5] A prominent obituary in *The New York Times* reported that his family gave his birthday as September 23, 1830, but that some published lists of actors' ages, "not always trustworthy", put his birth year at 1824.[10]

1.2.6 References

Notes

[1] Souvenir card given to Charles Warren Stoddard showing Edwards as an actor with the California Theatre Stock Company. The inscription reads:
"To my valued friend Chas. W. Stoddard -
with my most affectionate regards
San Francisco. Dec 9, 1871 Hy. Edwards."

[2] Beutenmuller, William (July 1899). "Henry Edwards". *The Canadian Entomologist* **23** (7): 141–142. doi:10.4039/Ent23141-7.

[3] Garnett, 1908, p. 7.

[4] Remington, J. E. (January 1948). "Henry Edwards (1830–1891)" (PDF). *The Lepidopterists' News* **II** (1): 7. Retrieved July 23, 2009.

[5] Brown-May and May, 1997

[6] Lawrence, W. J. (1892). "Chapter X: Australia. 1857–1861". *The life of Gustavus Vaughan Brooke, tragedian.* Belfast: W. & G. Baird. pp. 117, 196–204, 234.

[7] Edwards, Henry (1883). "Two Balloon Voyages". *A Mingled Yarn.* New York: G. P. Putnam's Sons. pp. 131–138.

[8] *The Transactions of the Entomological Society of London.* Royal Entomological Society of London. 1891. pp. li–lii.

[9] United States Census, 1870. San Francisco, 2d Precinct, 12th Ward, page 38. June 14, 1870.

[10] "Obituary: Henry Edwards, Comedian". *The New York Times*. June 10, 1891. Retrieved January 17, 2010.

[11] Knight, Joseph (September 2004). "Avonia Jones". *Oxford Dictionary of National Biography.* Oxford University Press. Retrieved February 16, 2010.

[12] Lawrence, 1892, pp. 274–277.

[13] Shuck, Oscar T. (1897). *Historical Abstract of San Francisco.* San Francisco: Oscar T. Shuck. p. 84. Retrieved January 8, 2010.

[14] Hendley, Alvis (2004). "Landmark 86: Site of The California Theatre.". *California Historical Landmarks in San Francisco.* NoeHill in San Francisco. Retrieved December 31, 2009.

[15] Leman, Walter M. (1886). *Memories of an Old Actor.* San Francisco: H. S. Crocker. pp. 359–360.

[16] Bohemian Club (1904). *Constitution, By-laws, and Rules, Officers, Committees, and Members*, pp. 19–20, 69.

[17] Garnett, 1908, p. 120.

[18] Badè, William Frederic (1924). *The Life and Letters of John Muir.* Boston and New York: Houghton Mifflin. pp. 262–264. Retrieved January 24, 2010.

[19] Holland, William Jacob (1903). *The Moth Book.* New York: Doubleday, Page & company. p. 249.

[20] Edwards, Henry (1875). "A Tribute to George Robert Crotch". *Proceedings of the California Academy of Sciences* (California Academy of Sciences): 332.

[21] "Obituary Notice: Henry Edwards". *Proceedings of the California Academy of Sciences* (California Academy of Sciences): 367. 1891.

[22] "The New Jinks and Old Jinks: Midnight Programmes in the Forest". *The San Francisco Call* (San Francisco). July 12, 1896. Retrieved January 25, 2010.

[23] Garnett, 1908, p. 6.

[24] Weiss, Philip (November 1989). "Masters of the Universe Go to Camp: Inside the Bohemian Grove." *Spy Magazine*, pp. 59–76. Hosted by University of California, Santa Cruz, Sociology Department, Professor G. William Domhoff. Retrieved on January 15, 2010.

[25] Tompkins, 1908, p. 258.

[26] Tompkins, 1908, p. 266.

[27] United States Census, 1880. Boston, Massachusetts, Enumeration District 772, Supervisor's District 60, page 29. June 8, 1880.

[28] Edwards, Henry (January 1884). "To Our Subscribers". *Papilio* (New York Entomological Club): 104.

[29] Hardee, Lewis (2006). *The Lambs Theatre Club.* Jefferson, North Carolina: McFarland. p. 47. ISBN 0-7864-2321-8.

[30] Kerr, Frederick (1930). *Recollections of a Defective Memory*. London: Thornton Butterworth. p. 40.

[31] Actors' Fund of America (1892). *Souvenir and programme of the Actors' Fund Fair, Madison Square Garden, May 2d, 3d, 4th, 5th, 6th, 7th, 1892*. New York: U. W. Pratt. pp. 63, 71.

[32] King1, Moses (1893). *Kings Handbook of New York* (2 ed.). Boston. pp. 592–593. Retrieved January 24, 2010.

[33] Edwards, Henry (1883). "Dedication". *A Mingled Yarn*. New York: G. P. Putnam's Sons. p. 3.

[34] Pylodet, L.; Augusta Harriet (Garrigue) Leypoldt (May 1883). "A Mingled Yarn: Extracts from N.Y. Tribune, April 3". *Literary News* (New York: F. Leypoldt) **IV** (5): 155.

[35] Harvier, Evelyn (August 30, 1886). "Harry Edwards at Home". *The Theatre* (New York: Theatre Publishing) **1** (24): 539–540.

[36] Archer, William (1889). Edward Fuller, ed. *The Dramatic Year 1887–1888*. Boston: Ticknor and Company. pp. 62, 72–74.

[37] "The Amusement Season; Dramatic and Musical. *Elaine* on the stage.". *The New York Times*. April 29, 1887. Retrieved January 28, 2010.

[38] Clapp, John B.; Edwin F. Edgett (1902). *Plays of the Present*. New York: The Dunlap Society. p. 97.

[39] Welch, Deshler (1888). *The Theatre* **III**. New York: Theatre Publishing Company. p. 148.

[40] Brown, Thomas Allston (1903). *A history of the New York stage from the first performance in 1732 to 1901* **3**. New York: Dodd, Mead and Company. pp. 325–328. Retrieved January 24, 2010.

[41] Hutton, Laurence (1889). "Preface". In Lester Wallack. *Memories of Fifty Years*. New York: Charles Scribner's Sons. p. viii.

[42] "Rare Butterflies and Moths.; Harry Edwards's Collection Will Soon Be On Exhibition.". *The New York Times*. April 10, 1892. Retrieved January 28, 2010.

[43] "Donations". *Annual Report of the American Museum of Natural History* (American Museum of Natural History). 20–24. 1892.

[44] Osborn, Henry Fairfield (1911). *The American Museum of Natural History: its origin, its history, the growth of its departments to December 31, 1909*. Chicago: Irving Press. p. 121.

[45] Department of Library Services (1999). "Library History". *About the Library*. American Museum of Natural History. Retrieved January 28, 2010.

[46] Edwards, Henry (February 19, 1881). "New Genera and Species of North American Noctuidae". *Papilio* (New York: New York Entomological Club) **1** (2): 19–20.

[47] Edwards, Henry (November 1881). "New Genera and Species of the Family Aegeridae". *Papilio* (New York: New York Entomological Club) **1** (10): 190.

[48] Oehlke, Bill. "Catocala: Classification and Common Names". The Catocala Website. Retrieved July 23, 2009.

[49] Silkmoths. *Catocala ophelia*. Retrieved on January 8, 2010.

[50] Silkmoths. *Catocala hermia*. Retrieved on January 8, 2010.

[51] Silkmoths. *Catocala desdemona*. Retrieved on January 8, 2010.

Bibliography

- Beutenmuller, William (December 1891). "List of Writings of the Late Henry Edwards". *The Canadian Entomologist* (London). XXIII (12): 259–267. doi:10.4039/Ent23259-12.

- Brown-May, Andrew; Tom W. May (June 1997). "'A Mingled Yarn': Henry Edwards, Thespian and Naturalist, in the Austral Land of Plenty, 1853–1866". *Historical Records of Australian Science* **11** (3): 407–418. doi:10.1071/hr9971130407.

- Garnett, Porter (1908). *The Bohemian Jinks: A Treatise*. San Francisco: The Bohemian Club.

- Tompkins, Eugene; Quincy Kilby (1908). *The history of the Boston Theatre, 1854–1901*. Boston: Houghton Mifflin Company.

1.2.7 External links

- Harry Edwards life mask

1.3 Bohemian Club

For other uses, see Bohemian Club (disambiguation).

The **Bohemian Club** is a private club in two locations: a city clubhouse in the Union Square district of San Francisco, California, and the Bohemian Grove, a retreat north of the city in Sonoma County.[3] Founded in 1872 from a regular meeting of journalists, artists and musicians, it soon began to accept businessmen and entrepreneurs as permanent members, as well as offering temporary membership to university presidents and military commanders who were serving in the San Francisco Bay Area. Today, the club has a diverse membership of many local and global leaders, ranging from artists and musicians to businessmen.

1.3.1 Clubhouse

The Bohemian Club's City Clubhouse, viewed from the corner of Taylor Street and Post Street.

The Bohemian Club has two locations: the City Club and the Bohemian Grove (see below). The City Club is located in a six-story masonry building at the corner of Post Street and Taylor Street, two blocks west of Union Square, and on the same block as both the Olympic Club and the Marines Memorial Club. The clubhouse contains dining rooms, meeting rooms, a bar, a library, an art gallery, a theater, and guestrooms.

1.3.2 History

Bohemianism

Main article: Bohemianism

In New York City and other American metropolises in the late 1850s, groups of young, cultured journalists flourished as self-described "bohemians" until the American Civil War broke them up and sent them out as war correspondents.[4] During the war, reporters began to assume the title "bohemian," and newspapermen in general took up the moniker. "Bohemian" became synonymous with "newspaper writer".[4] California journalist Bret Harte first wrote as "The Bohemian" in *The Golden Era* in 1861, with this persona taking part in many satirical doings. Harte described San Francisco as a sort of Bohemia of the West.[5] Mark Twain called himself and poet Charles Warren Stoddard bohemians in 1867.[4]

Founding

The Bohemian Club was originally formed in April 1872 by and for journalists who wished to promote a fraternal con-

nection among men who enjoyed the arts. Michael Henry de Young, proprietor of the *San Francisco Chronicle*, provided this description of its formation in a 1915 interview:

> The Bohemian Club was organized in the *Chronicle* office by Tommy Newcombe, Sutherland, Dan O'Connell, Harry Dam and others who were members of the staff. The boys wanted a place where they could get together after work, and they took a room on Sacramento street below Kearny. That was the start of the Bohemian Club, and it was not an unmixed blessing for the Chronicle because the boys would go there sometimes when they should have reported at the office. Very often when Dan O'Connell sat down to a good dinner there he would forget that he had a pocketful of notes for an important story.[6]

Journalists were to be regular members; artists and musicians were to be honorary members.[7] The group quickly relaxed its rules for membership to permit some people to join who had little artistic talent, but enjoyed the arts and had greater financial resources. Eventually, the original "bohemian" members were in the minority and the wealthy and powerful controlled the club.[8][9] Club members who were established and successful, respectable family men, defined for themselves their own form of bohemianism which included men who were bons vivants, sometime outdoorsmen, and appreciators of the arts.[5] Club member and poet George Sterling responded to this redefinition:

> Any good mixer of convivial habits considers he has a right to be called a Bohemian. But that is not a valid claim. There are two elements, at least, that are essential to Bohemianism. The first is devotion or addiction to one or more of the Seven Arts; the other is poverty. Other factors suggest themselves: for instance, I like to think of my Bohemians as young, as radical in their outlook on art and life; as unconventional, and, though this is debatable, as dwellers in a city large enough to have the somewhat cruel atmosphere of all great cities.[10]

Despite his purist views, Sterling associated very closely with the Bohemian Club, and caroused with artist and industrialist alike at the Bohemian Grove.[10]

Oscar Wilde, upon visiting the club in 1882, is reported to have said "I never saw so many well-dressed, well-fed, business-looking Bohemians in my life."[11]

Membership

A number of past membership lists are in public domain,[7] but modern club membership lists are private. Some prominent figures have been given honorary membership, such as Richard Nixon and William Randolph Hearst. Members have included some U.S. presidents (usually before they are elected to office), many cabinet officials, and CEOs of large corporations, including major financial institutions. Major military contractors, oil companies, banks (including the Federal Reserve), utilities, and national media have high-ranking officials as club members or guests. Many members are, or have been, on the board of directors of several of these corporations; however, artists and lovers of art are among the most active members. The club's bylaws require ten percent of the membership be accomplished artists of all types (composers, musicians, singers, actors, lighting artists, painters, authors, etc.)

The club motto is "Weaving Spiders Come Not Here", a line taken from Act 2, Scene 2, of Shakespeare's *A Midsummer Night's Dream*. The club motto implies that outside concerns and business deals are to be left outside. When gathered in groups, Bohemians usually adhere to the injunction, though discussion of business often occurs between pairs of members.[12]

1.3.3 Bohemian Grove

Main article: Bohemian Grove

Every year the club hosts a two-week-long (three week-

The club's mascot owl cast in masonry perched over the main entrance at 624 Taylor. The owl is flanked by the letters B and C and surrounded by words of the club's motto

ends) camp at Bohemian Grove, which is notable for its illustrious guest list and its eclectic *Cremation of Care* cere-

mony which mockingly burns "Care" (the normal woes of life) with grand pageantry, pyrotechnics and brilliant costumes, all done at the edge of a lake and at the base of a forty-foot 'stone' owl statue. In addition to that ceremony, there are also two outdoor performances (dramatic and comedic plays), often with elaborate set design and orchestral accompaniment. The more elaborate of the two is the Grove Play, or *High Jinks*, the more ribald is called *Low Jinks*.[13] More often than not, the productions are original creations of the Associate members but active participation of hundreds of members of all backgrounds is traditional.[14]

1.3.4 Bret Harte Memorial

The Bret Harte Memorial by Jo Mora.

A bronze relief by Jo Mora is installed on the exterior of the building. It serves as a memorial to author and poet Bret Harte. The relief, which is approximately 3 ft. 3 7/8 in. x 7 ft. 11 5/8 in. x 2 1/2 in. (101 cm x 243 cm x 6 cm), was first dedicated in on August 15, 1919, as a tribute by Mora, who was a member, to fellow Bohemian Club member Harte. The relief shows fifteen characters from books by Harte. It is inscribed:

Proper left, upper corner:

> J J MORA
> AUGUST 15, 1919

Proper left, lower edge:

> L. DE ROME
> BRONZE FOUNDRY

Top center wreath:

> IN

MEMORIAM

BRET

HARTE

1836–1902

AD

followed by the founder's mark for L. De Rome. When the original building was torn down, the relief was removed. In 1934, it was reinstalled on the building that stands today.[15]

1.3.5 See also

- List of American gentlemen's clubs

- List of Bohemian Club members

- Belizean Grove – Women's only club in New York City modeled after the Bohemian Grove

- The Family (club)

- Membership discrimination in California social clubs

1.3.6 References

Notes

[1] "Social clubs".

[2] http://nccsdataweb.urban.org/orgs/profile/940331150?popup=1

[3] Kay, Jane (July 6, 2009). "No retreat from uproar over Bohemian Club woods". *San Francisco Chronicle*. Retrieved 14 July 2009.

[4] The Mark Twain Project. Explanatory Notes regarding the letter from Samuel Langhorne Clemens to Charles Warren Stoddard, 23 Apr 1867. Retrieved on July 26, 2009.

[5] Ogden, Dunbar H.; Douglas McDermott; Robert Károly Sarlós *Theatre West: Image and Impact*, Rodopi, 1990, pp. 17–42. ISBN 90-5183-125-0

[6] Interview with Michael Henry De Young, 1915, reproduced at https://archive.org/stream/variedtypes00odayrich/variedtypes00odayrich_djvu.txt.

[7] *The Elite directory for San Francisco and Oakland*, Argonaut Publishing Co., 1879, pp. 175–184.

[8] Bohemian Club. *Constitution, By-laws, and Rules, Officers, Committees, and Members*, Bohemian Club, 1904, p. 11. *Semi-centennial high jinks in the Grove, 1922*, Bohemian Club, 1922, pp. 11–22.

[9] Parry, 2005, pp. 218–219.

[10] Parry, 2005, p. 238.

[11] Finn, Maria (October 9, 2010). "Keeping Reality at Bay". Wall Street Journal.

[12] Peter Martin Phillips, A Relative Advantage: Sociology of the San Francisco Bohemian Club, 1994.

[13] Garnett, 1908.

[14] Domhoff, 1975.

[15] "Bret Harte Memorial, (sculpture)". *Save Outdoor Sculpture!*. Smithsonian American Art Museum. Retrieved 2012-05-09.

Bibliography

- Bohemian Club. *Constitution, By-laws, and Rules, Officers, Committees, and Members*, 1904

- Bohemian Club. *Semi-centennial high jinks in the Grove*, July 28, 1922. Haig Patigian, Sire.

- Bohemian Club. *History, officers and committees, incorporation, constitution, by-laws and rules, former officers, members, in memoriam*, 1960

- Bohemian Club. *History, officers and committees, incorporation, constitution, by-laws and rules, former officers, members, in memoriam*, 1962

- Domhoff, G. William. *Bohemian Grove and Other Retreats: A Study in Ruling-Class Cohesiveness*, Harper & Row, 1975. ISBN 0-06-131880-9

- Dulfer & Hoag. *Our Society Blue Book*, San Francisco, Dulfer & Hoag, 1925.

- Garnett, Porter, *The Bohemian Jinks: A Treatise*, 1908

- Ogden, Dunbar H.; Douglas McDermott; Robert Károly Sarlós (1990). *Theatre West: Image and Impact*. Rodopi. ISBN 90-5183-125-0.

- Parry, Albert. (2005.) *Garretts & Pretenders: A History of Bohemianism in America*, Cosimo, Inc. ISBN 1-59605-090-X

Coordinates: 37°47′17″N 122°24′42″W / 37.78814°N 122.41160°W

1.4 Cremation of Care

The **Cremation of Care** is an annual theatrical production written, produced and performed by and for members of the Bohemian Club, and staged at the Bohemian Grove near

THE CREMATION OF CARE (1907)

The pyrotechnic climax to the 1907 Cremation of Care

Monte Rio, California at a small artificial lake amid a private old-growth grove of Redwood trees.

The dramatic performance is presented on the first night of the annual encampment[1] as an allegorical banishing of worldly cares for the club members, and "to present symbolically the salvation of the trees by the club",[2] but the secretive nature of the Bohemians, and the political power of some of its members, has attracted notice from conspiracy theorists such as Alex Jones, who characterized the *Cremation of Care* as a ritualistic shedding of conscience and empathy, and an "abuse of power".[3]

1.4.1   History

In 1878, the Bohemian Club of San Francisco first took to the woods in Taylorville, California (present-day Samuel P. Taylor State Park) for a summer celebration that they called Midsummer High Jinks.[4] Poems were recited, songs were sung, and dramatic readings were given; the practice was repeated each summer in other areas, primarily near the Russian River in Sonoma County. In 1881, the ceremony of the *Cremation of Care* was first conducted after the various individual performances, with James F. Bowman as Sire.[5] The ceremony was further expanded in 1893 by a member named Joseph D. Redding,[6] with a Midsummer High Jinks entitled *The Sacrifice in the Forest*, or simply "Druid Jinks", in which brotherly love and Christianity battled and won against paganism, converting the druids away from bloody sacrifice.[7] Redding formed the framework of the ceremony but the main actors, including George Tisdale Bromley as High Priest, were asked to supply their own major speeches.[7] In 1904, the prologue to William Henry Irwin's Grove Play *The Hamadryads* included text such as "Touch their world-blind eyes with fairy unguents." The play depicted the intrusion, the battles, and the symbolic death of the maleficent Spirit of Care.[8]

In the earliest productions of the Grove Play, several restrictions were imposed upon the Sire (the master of ceremonies[9]) including that the stage setting be the natural forest backdrop and that the "malign character Care" be introduced in the plot, to wreak havoc with the characters and then be faced down and vanquished by the hero.[2] In these early productions, the *Cremation of Care* immediately followed, and lasted until midnight.[10] The end of the ceremony was signaled by a lively Jinks Band rendition of *There'll Be a Hot Time in the Old Town Tonight*,[11] and the club members sat down to a late dinner and revelry.[12]

From 1913, the *Cremation of Care* was disengaged from the Grove Play, and rescheduled for the first night of the summer encampment.[1] The Grove Play was set for the final weekend.[1] A different Sire was appointed for the Cremation, and some concerns were raised in subsequent years that the *Cremation of Care* was growing into its own secondary Grove Play. Some Sires experimented with a satirical treatment, or topical themes such as a patriotic World War I treatment in 1918 and an unpopular Prohibition script in 1919. "Care" was not killed, let alone cremated, in the 1922 version. In response to member complaints about the unpredictable quality of the opening night fare, Charles K. Field was asked in 1923 to standardize the script for what became the basis for every subsequent *Cremation of Care* ceremony.[13]

1.4.2   Staging

The Owl Shrine covered in moss, standing among trees behind a stage at one edge of a man-made pond.

The ceremony involves the poling across a lake of a small boat containing an effigy of Care (called "Dull Care"). Dark, hooded figures receive from the ferryman the effigy which is placed on an altar, and, at the end of the ceremony, set on fire. This "cremation" symbolizes that members are banishing the "dull cares" of conscience.[14] At the time the script was developed, the primary meaning of the word 'care' (< O.E. *cearu*, "anxiety, anguish") was synonymous with 'worry', having more negative connotations than in modern times when it tends to be associated more positively with compassion.[15]

The ceremony takes place in front of the Owl Shrine, a 40-foot (12 m) hollow owl statue made of concrete over steel supports. The moss- and lichen-covered statue simulates a natural rock formation, yet holds electrical and audio equipment within it. During the ceremony, a recording is used as the voice of The Owl. For many years the recorded voice was club guest Walter Cronkite.[16] Music and pyrotechnics accompany the ritual for dramatic effect.[17][18][19][20]

1.4.3 Controversy

On July 15, 2000, Austin, Texas-based filmmaker Alex Jones and his cameraman, Mike Hanson, infiltrated the Bohemian Grove expecting to uncover the owl statue being worshipped as Moloch, with human sacrifices thrown into its fiery interior.[3] With a hidden camera, Jones and Hanson were able to film the *Cremation of Care* ceremony. The footage was the centerpiece of Jones' documentary *Dark Secrets: Inside Bohemian Grove*. Jones claimed that the *Cremation of Care* was an "ancient Canaanite, Luciferian, Babylon mystery religion ceremony". The Grove and Jones' investigation were covered by Jon Ronson in Channel 4's four-part documentary *Secret Rulers of the World*. Ronson documented his view of the ritual in his book *Them: Adventures with Extremists*, writing: "My lasting impression was of an all-pervading sense of immaturity: the Elvis impersonators, the pseudo-pagan spooky rituals, the heavy drinking. These people might have reached the apex of their professions but emotionally they seemed trapped in their college years."[21]

Protests

Outside of the main entrance to the Bohemian Grove, protesters against club members and their guests have held a ceremony called the "Resurrection of Care", intended to symbolically reverse the effects of the Cremation of Care, to prevent the attendees from temporarily abandoning their cares.[16] The counter ceremony was first held in 1980, organized by Mary Moore, a former beauty queen turned left-wing activist. Moore was less concerned about the Cremation of Care ceremony than with the likelihood that club members with corporate interests would gain influence in government.[22]

1.4.4 References

Notes

[1] Garnett, 1908, p. 36.

[2] Garnett, 1908, p. 25.

[3] Jones, Alex. *Dark Secrets: Inside Bohemian Grove*. 2000.

[4] Garnett, 1908, p. ix.

[5] Garnett, 1908, pp. 19–20.

[6] Domhoff, 1974.

[7] Garnett, 1908, p. 21.

[8] Garnett, 1908, pp. 4–5.

[9] Garnett, 1908, p. 17.

[10] Garnett, 1908, p. 27.

[11] Ogden, 1990, p. 25.

[12] Garnett, 1908, p. 30.

[13] Garnett, 1908, pp. 37–39.

[14] Phillips, 1994.

[15] "History of the Notion of Care", *Encyclopedia of Bioethics* (1995)

[16] Philip Weiss, Masters of the Universe Go to Camp: Inside the Bohemian Grove. *Spy Magazine*, November 1989

[17] Sir George Grove, Waldo Selden Pratt, Charles Newell Boyd, ed. (1920). *Grove's Dictionary of Music and Musicians* **6**. Macmillan. p. 136.

[18] Miller, Leta E. (2011). *Music and Politics in San Francisco: From the 1906 Quake to the Second World War*. University of California Press. p. 38. ISBN 9780520268913.

[19] Wert, Hal Elliott (2005). *Hoover The Fishing President: Portrait of the Private Man and His Life Outdoors*. Stackpole Books. p. 108. ISBN 9780811700993.

[20] Buck, Richard P.; Bethards, Jack M. (2005). *Music and Musicians in Bohemia: The First One Hundred Years – a Research Document*. Bohemian Club. p. 389.

[21] Ronson, Jon (2002). *Them: Adventures with Extremists*. Simon and Schuster. p. 321. ISBN 0-7432-3321-2. Retrieved 2010-04-18.

[22] Barry, Dan (July 27, 2010). "Redwoods Hideaway for the Elite Goes On, but Protest Days Fade". *The New York Times*. Retrieved June 29, 2011.

Bibliography

- Bohemian Club. *Cremation of Care, Bohemian Club Grove*, 1914

- Bohemian Club. *Ceremony of the Cremation of Care*, July 27, 1918

- Bohemian Club. *History, officers and committees, incorporation, constitution, by-laws and rules, former officers, members, in memoriam*, 1960

- Bohemian Club. *History, officers and committees, incorporation, constitution, by-laws and rules, former officers, members, in memoriam*, 1962

- Bromley, George T.; Frederick Somers; Bohemian Club. *The Cremation of Care Fifty-third Celebration*, 1933

- Domhoff, G. William, *The Bohemian Grove and Other Retreats: A study in ruling class cohesiveness*, Harper and Row, 1974.

- Field, Charles Kellogg; Bohemian Club. *The Cremation of Care.* "On the Occasion of the Sixty-seventh Consecutive Performance of the Cremation of Care, the Ritual Now in Use is Published by the Club for Its Members with the Introductory Review of the Evolution of the Ceremonial." 1947

- Field, Palmer; Bohemian Club. *The Cremation of Care: A History Exhumed and Dusted Off by Palmer Field.* "Upon the Occasion of the 74th Consecutive Performance, July 18, 1953"

- Garnett, Porter, *The Bohemian Jinks: A Treatise*, 1908

- Keeler, Charles Augustus; Wade C Hughan; Karen Melcher (frontispiece); Peter Rutledge Koch. *A Service for the Cremation of Care*, Lands End Press, 1989

- Newhall, Almer M.; Bohemian Club. *The Ceremony of the Cremation of Care*, 1920

- Ogden, Dunbar H.; Douglas McDermott; Robert Károly Sarlós (1990). *Theatre West: Image and Impact*. Rodopi. ISBN 90-5183-125-0.

- Phillips, Peter Martin. *A Relative Advantage: Sociology of the San Francisco Bohemian Club*, 1994.

- Swinnerton, James G.; Bohemian Club. *The Cremation of Care.* "Fiftieth anniversary of the cremation of care." 1930

1.5 List of Bohemian Club members

The following **list of Bohemian Club members** includes both past and current members of note. Membership in the male-only, private Bohemian Club takes a variety of forms, with membership regularly offered to new university presidents and to military commanders stationed in the San Francisco Bay Area. Regular, full members are usually

The Bohemian Club's mascot is an owl, here cast in masonry, and perched over the main club entrance at 624 Taylor Street in San Francisco.

wealthy and influential men who pay full membership fees and dues, and who must often wait 15 years for an opening, as the club limits itself to about 2700 men. Associate members are graphic and musical artists, and actors, who pay lesser fees because of their usefulness in assisting with club activities in San Francisco and at the Bohemian Grove. Professional members are associate members who have developed the ability to pay full dues, or are skilled professionals selected from the arts community.

Honorary members are elected by club members, and pay no membership fees or annual dues. Four women were made honorary members in the club's first two decades, though they were not given the full privileges of regular club members.[1] Several honorary members never availed themselves of the club's offer—there is no record of Mark Twain visiting the club, and Boston resident Oliver Wendell Holmes never visited but he responded immediately with a poem when notified by telegram of the honor, despite being wakened at midnight.[2]

Each member is associated with a "camp", that is, one of 118 rustic sleeping and leisure quarters scattered throughout the Bohemian Grove, where each member sleeps during the two weeks (three weekends) of annual summer encampment in July. These camps are the principal means through which high-level business and political contacts and friendships are formed.[3]

1.5.1 References

Notes

[1] Ogden, Dunbar H.; Douglas McDermott; Robert Károly

Sarlós (1990). *Theatre West: Image and Impact*. Rodopi. p. 36. ISBN 90-5183-125-0.

[2] Morse, John Torrey (1899). *Life and letters of Oliver Wendell Holmes* **1**. Houghton, Mifflin. p. 249.

[3] Peter Martin Phillips, A Relative Advantage: Sociology of the San Francisco Bohemian Club, 1994.

[4] Bohemian Club Constitution, 1904

[5] Trower, W. P. (2009). *Luis Walter Alvarez 1911–1988* (PDF). Biographical Memoirs. National Academy of Sciences. Retrieved March 21, 2013.

[6] Rove, Karl (2010). *Courage and Consequence: My Life as a Conservative in the Fight*. Simon and Schuster. p. 344. ISBN 9781439199268.

[7] Wilson, Mark (2011). *Bernard Maybeck*. Gibbs Smith. p. 175. ISBN 9781423611813.

[8] *Oakland Magazine*, March 2007. Matt Dibble, *The Life and Times of the Oakland Song*. Retrieved on July 14, 2009.

[9] Domhoff, G. William. *Social Cohesion & the Bohemian Grove: The Power Elite at Summer Camp*, April 2005. Retrieved on July 20, 2009.

[10] Lekisch, Barbara (2003). *Embracing Scenes about Lakes Tahoe & Donner: Painters, Illustrators & Sketch Artists 1855–1915*. Great West Books. p. 20. ISBN 9780944220146.

[11] San Francisco Social Register, 1927.

[12] Bohemian Club, 1960

[13] Fletcher, Robert H. (1898). *Annals of the Bohemian Club*. The Bohemian Club.

[14] Social register: *San Francisco, including Oakland*, 1918.

[15] Bohemian Club, 1922

[16] Grove's Dictionary of Music and Musicians. *Life*, No. 17 of the 'Grove-Plays'. Retrieved on June 30, 2009.

[17] Music Library Association, Northern California Chapter. MLA NCC Newsletter, Vol. 16, no. 2 (Spring 2002). John L. Walker, Bringing the Masses to the Music: Ulderico Marcelli and the Silent Film in San Francisco. Retrieved on June 29, 2009.

[18] St. Mary's College of California. Hearst Art Gallery. *Early Artists of the Bohemian Club*. Retrieved on March 29, 2014.

[19] Sancton, Julian (April 1, 2009). "A Guide to the Bohemian Grove". *Vanity Fair* (vanityfair.com). Retrieved December 21, 2010.

[20] Music Library Association, Northern California Chapter. Newsletter, Fall 2003. Michelle Squyer, *Beyond Measure: L.S. Sherman and Sherman, Clay & Company, A San Francisco House of Music, 1870-1926*. Retrieved on July 23, 2009.

[21] Bohemian Club Constitution, 1895

[22] Morain, Dan (May 26, 1987). "Bohemian Club Unyielding : Bastion of the Powerful Clings to Male Mystique". *Los Angeles Times*.

[23] *Who's Running America?: The Conservative Years*. Pearson Education Canada. 1986. p. 215.

[24] Coutts caricature of Herman George Scheffauer, photograph by Gabriel Moulin, Bohemian Grove 1908. Online Archive of California.

[25] Starr, Kevin (1996). *Endangered Dreams: The Great Depression in California*. Oxford University Press. p. 139. ISBN 9780195100808.

[26] Ryder, David Warren (1962). *'Great Citizen': A Biography of William H. Crocker*. Historical Publications. p. 190.

[27] Serrano, Richard A.; Savage, David G. (December 31, 2004). "Justice Thomas Reports Wealth of Gifts: In the last six years he has accepted free items valued at $42,200, the most on the high court". *Los Angeles Times*. p. 3.

[28] McIntire, Mike (June 18, 2011). "Friendship of Justice and Magnate Puts Focus on Ethics". *The New York Times*.

[29] Lekisch 2003, p. 53.

[30] San Francisco Genealogy. Obits. "Da - Dg". Retrieved on July 21, 2009.

[31] "Obituary – Bobby Enriquez". *San Francisco Chronicle*. August 10, 1996.

[32] Evans, Richard B.; Donald L. Winks; Adrian McNamara; Bohemian Club. *Tyburn Fair*, Bohemian Club, 1991.

[33] Syukhtun Editions. Theo Radic, *Manuel Y. Ferrer*. Retrieved on July 21, 2009.

[34] San Francisco Genealogy. Bohemian Club Officers and Members, 1905. Retrieved on July 23, 2009.

[35] Garnett, 1908.

[36] Drew, Elizabeth (1995). *On the Edge: The Clinton Presidency*. Simon and Schuster. p. 370. ISBN 9780684813097. Gergen resigned his membership in 1993 when he joined the Clinton presidential team.

[37] Bohemian Club, 1973

[38] Lekisch 2003, p. 77.

[39] Lekisch 2003, p. 81.

[40] Lekisch 2003, p. 93.

[41] Lekisch 2003, p. 94.

[42] "In Memoriam: Charles D. Hollister". Woods Hole Oceanographic Institute. August 25, 1999. Retrieved April 13, 2010.

[43] Starr 1996, p. 293

[44] San Francisco Genealogy. Obits. "Hs - Hz". Retrieved on July 21, 2009.

[45] Thorpe, James Ernest. *Henry Edwards Huntington: a biography*, University of California Press, 1994, p. 127. ISBN 0-520-08254-0

[46] Drew 1995, pp. 370–372

[47] "The Midsummer Music of Bohemia". *Pacific Coast Musical Review* **34**: 4.

[48] Nachman, Gerald. *The Columnist*, May 10, 2006. "Timidity and dull writing helping kill newspapers". Retrieved on July 14, 2009.

[49] Kinnaird, Lawrence (1966). *History of the Greater San Francisco Bay Region* **3**. Lewis Historical Publishing Company. p. 321.

[50] Reagan, Ronald (2004). *Reagan: A Life In Letters*. Simon and Schuster. p. 122. ISBN 9780743219679.

[51] Schevitz, Tanya (June 24, 2011). "George Lenczowski – UC Professor, Middle East Expert". *San Francisco Chronicle* (SFGate.com). Retrieved July 10, 2012.

[52] Pinchard, 1922, pp. 222–233

[53] Bohemian Club. *The Rout of the Philistines, A Forest Play* (1922).

[54] Bohemian Club. *Aloha Oe: a Legend of Hawaii* (1958).

[55] Marston, Otis R., (2014). "From Powell To Power; A Recounting of the First One Hundred River Runners Through the Grand Canyon. Flagstaff, Arizona: Vishnu Temple Press, p. 531 ISBN 978-0990527022

[56] Gale, Phil, (2011). The Marstons in Berkeley Part 2: The Children. Exactly Opposite, The Newsletter of the Berkeley Historical Society, Vol 29, No 1 Spring 2011

[57] ArchitectDB – architect record id 368: Clarence W. W. Mayhew

[58] Buck, Richard P.; Bethards, Jack M. (2005). *Music and Musicians in Bohemia: The First One Hundred Years: a Research Document*. The Bohemian Club.

[59] Brittain, Amy (March 7, 2006). "An Elite Alliance – Chancellor confirms membership in club". *The Daily Reveille* (Louisiana State University). Archived from the original on February 9, 2007. Retrieved May 13, 2014.

[60] Poletti, Therese; Tom Paiva (2008). *Art Deco San Francisco: The Architecture of Timothy Pflueger*. Princeton Architectural Press. p. 14. ISBN 1-56898-756-0.

[61] *Congressional Directory*. United States Congress. 1915. p. 8.

[62] Starr, Kevin. *Material Dreams: Southern California through the 1920s*, Oxford University Press US, 1990, p. 276. ISBN 0-19-504487-8

[63] Weir, Bob. , Bohemian Grove Secrets and Stories Told by Bob Weir

[64] Social register: *San Francisco*, 1920.

[65] Rhodes, William Henry; edited by Daniel O'Connell. *Caxton's Book: A Collection of Essays, Poems, Tales and Sketches*, A. L. Bancroft, 1876

[66] Shoup Papers archived at Stanford Library Retrieved on March 26, 2014.

[67] San Francisco Genealogy. Obits. "Tg - Tl". Retrieved on July 21, 2009.

[68] Maher, Michael J. *John Charles Thomas: beloved baritone of American opera and popular music*, McFarland, 2006, pp. 17, 120–125, 136, 160. ISBN 0-7864-2668-3

[69] California School for the Deaf. History: *Douglas Tilden*. Retrieved on July 21, 2009.

[70] Lekisch 2003, p. 215.

[71] *SF Weekly*, July 29, 1998. Silke Tudor, "Night Crawler". Retrieved on July 22, 2009.

Bibliography

• Bohemian Club. *Constitution and by-laws of the Bohemian Club of San Francisco*, 1895

• Bohemian Club. *Constitution, By-laws, and Rules, Officers, Committees, and Members*, 1904

• Bohemian Club. *Semi-centennial high jinks in the Grove*, July 28, 1922. Haig Patigian, Sire.

• Bohemian Club. *History, officers and committees, incorporation, constitution, by-laws and rules, former officers, members, in memoriam*, 1960

• Bohemian Club. *History, officers and committees, incorporation, constitution, by-laws and rules, former officers, members, in memoriam*, 1962

• Bohemian Club. *History, officers and committees, former officers, in memoriam, house rules, Grove rules*, 1973

• Domhoff, G. William. *Bohemian Grove and Other Retreats: A Study in Ruling-Class Cohesiveness*, Harper & Row, 1975. ISBN 0-06-131880-9

• Dulfer & Hoag. *Our Society Blue Book*, San Francisco, Dulfer & Hoag, 1925.

- Garnett, Porter, *The Bohemian Jinks: A Treatise*, 1908

- Ogden, Dunbar H.; Douglas McDermott; Robert Károly Sarlós (1990). *Theatre West: Image and Impact*. Rodopi. ISBN 90-5183-125-0.

- Pinchard, Marguerite M. *The New society blue book; San Francisco, Oakland, Piedmont, Alameda*, 1922, pp. 222–233.

- Scheffauer, Herman George; Arthur Weiss; Bohemian Club. *The Sons of Baldur*, Bohemian Club, 1908.

- Social Register. San Francisco Social Register, 1927. B

- Stephens, Henry Morse; Wallace Arthur Sabin, Charles Caldwell Dobie, Bohemian Club. *St. Patrick at Tara*, 1909 Grove play

- Wilson, Harry Leon; Domenico Brescia; Bohemian Club. *Life*, Bohemian Club, 1919.

1.6   List of Grove Plays

The **Grove Play** is an annual theatrical production written, produced and performed by and for Bohemian Club members, and staged outdoors in California at the Bohemian Grove each summer.

In 1878, the Bohemian Club of San Francisco first took to the woods for a summer celebration that they called midsummer High Jinks.[1] Poems were recited, songs were sung, and dramatic readings were given. In 1881, the ceremony of the *Cremation of Care* was first conducted after the various individual performances.[2] Eventually, the readings and songs were woven into a theme or framework, such as in the solemn Orientalism-themed *Buddha Jinks* of 1892 and the Christianity-triumphs-over-paganism-themed *Druid Jinks* the next year.[3] In 1897, the *Faust Jinks* were constructed within the musical form of Charles Gounod's opera *Faust*.[4] Finally, in 1902, both the music and the libretto were composed by club members, setting the "Bohemian grove-play as a distinct genre of stage art."[4]

Each year a Sire and a musical Sire are selected by the club's Jinks Committee, part of the club's Board of Directors.[5] The Sire is responsible for producing the script and libretto of the Grove Play, and the musical Sire composes the music. The Sire may select others to write the dialog and song lyrics, but remains responsible for the overall theme and final form of the spectacle.

In the earliest productions of the Grove Play, several restrictions were imposed upon the Sire including that the stage setting be the natural forest backdrop and that the "malign

ST. PATRICK AT TARA
THE APPARITION OF CUCHULAINN

Maynard Dixon's illustration of the 1909 Grove Play St. Patrick at Tara, *showing the spirit of Irish hero Cuchulainn appearing to Saint Patrick among the Redwood trees of Northern California*

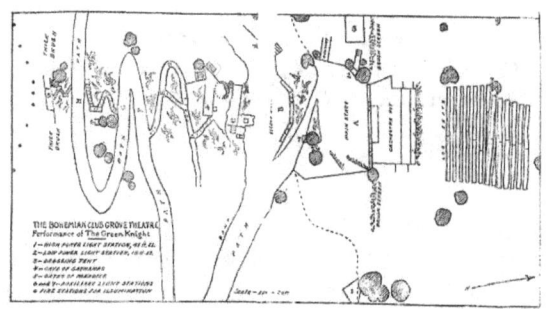

A 1911 sketch of the Grove Play stage, showing extensive upstage pathways and platforms amid the ferns and redwood trees

character Care" be introduced in the plot, to wreak havoc with the characters and then be faced down and vanquished by the hero.[6] In these early productions, the *Cremation of Care* immediately followed, and lasted until midnight.[7] The end of the ceremony was signaled by a lively Jinks

Band rendition of *There'll Be a Hot Time in the Old Town Tonight*,[8] and the club members sat down to a late dinner and revelry into the wee hours.[9]

From 1913, the *Cremation of Care* was disengaged from the Grove Play, and rescheduled for the first night of the summer encampment. The Grove Play was set for the final weekend.[10] A different Sire was appointed for the Cremation, and some concerns were raised in subsequent years that the *Cremation of Care* was growing into its own secondary Grove Play. Some Sires experimented with a satirical treatment, or topical themes such as a patriotic World War I treatment in 1918 and an unpopular Prohibition script in 1919. "Care" was not killed, let alone cremated, in the 1922 version. In response to member complaints about the unpredictable quality of the opening night fare, Charles K. Field was asked in 1923 to write the script for what became the basis for every subsequent *Cremation of Care* ceremony.[11]

A 1909 photograph of the dress rehearsal of St. Patrick at Tara, *showing the natural forest setting including switchback pathways extending the stage rearward up a hillside*

From 1902 to 1923, a central theme of most Grove Plays was the mystique of the ancient Coast Redwood tree grove.[12] Jack London wrote *The Acorn Planter: A California Forest Play* for the High Jinks but it was never staged; it was described as too difficult to set to music.[13] Beginning around 1920 with the installation of a large Austin pipe organ, the productions became more professional in tone.[14] In 1922, a sophisticated lighting system was installed at the Main Stage, the venue for the Grove Play.[1] During the World War II years 1943–1945, no Grove Plays were staged.

Unusual performances include the 1906 production of *The Owl and Care*, which is listed in Grove's dictionary as "Not strictly a Grove-Play."[15] *The Triumph of Bohemia* was already planned, but the 1906 San Francisco earthquake changed the club's priorities in favor of a more elabo-

rate cremation ceremony called *The Owl and Care*.[15] Two plays have been staged twice for the club members: *St. Patrick at Tara* in 1909 and 1934, and *A Gest of Robin Hood* in 1929 and 1954. 1912's *The Atonement of Pan* was performed once for club members and again two weeks later for members' wives and women friends. In 2008, the treatment of *The Count of Monte Cristo* was staged even though it had been published four years prior.

The cast for a Grove Play averages 75–100 actors, many appearing as so-called "spear carriers" in crowd scenes.[16] Roles for female characters are played by men,[17] since women are not allowed as members of the Bohemian Club. Including orchestra members, costumers, stage crew and carpenters, some 300 people are involved with the production each year.[18] The cost of each play was reported in the range of $20,000–30,000 in 1975, as much as $131,000 in current value. No salaries are given to club members who take part and no admission is charged the audience.[18] Rehearsals begin a year in advance.[18]

Observers have characterized the Grove Plays as massive, predictable and slow. Author John van der Zee has described the Grove Plays as "lumbering pageants."[19] Commenting on the plot, he said, "We know in advance that the hero will be a king or commander adored by his men, and that he will see his duty and do it."[19] Journalist Philip Weiss, writing in 1989 for *Spy* magazine, said that the high point of the two-week summer encampment was the "vigorously lowbrow" Low Jinks, a musical comedy staged during the middle weekend, not the "mannered and ponderous Grove Play."[20] Journalism professor Richard Reinhardt argued in 1980 that the showy bombast of Broadway theatre producer David Belasco helped form in the early Grove Plays a taste for majestic and astounding visual effects, and that this aesthetic sense has continued to the present in a form of "institutional inertia."[21]

1.6.1 References

Notes

[1] Ogden, 1990, p. 28.

[2] Garnett, 1908, pp. 19–20.

[3] Garnett, 1908, pp. 20–21.

[4] Garnett, 1908, p. 22.

[5] Garnett, 1908, p. 23.

[6] Garnett, 1908, p. 25.

[7] Garnett, 1908, p. 27.

[8] Ogden, 1990, p. 25.

[9] Garnett, 1908, p. 30.

[10] Garnett, 1908, p. 36.

[11] Garnett, 1908, pp. 37–39.

[12] Ogden, 1990, p. 19.

[13] Taylor, J. Golden. *A Literary history of the American West*, Western Literature Association, TCU Press, 1987, p. 394. ISBN 0-87565-021-X

[14] Ogden, 1990, p. 30.

[15] Pratt, Waldo Selden; George Grove; Charles Newell Boyd; John Alexander Fuller-Maitland. *Grove's dictionary of music and musicians*, Volume Six, 1920, p. 221.

[16] Newman, David M. *Sociology: Exploring the Architecture of Everyday Life : Readings*, SAGE Publications, 1999, p. 234. ISBN 0-7619-8655-3

[17] Ogden, 1990, p. 35.

[18] Domhoff, 1975, p. 10.

[19] SFGate.com, July 18, 2004. Adair Lara, *Members only: S.F.'s exclusive clubs carry on traditions of fellowship, culture -- and discrimination.* Retrieved on June 29, 2009.

[20] Philip Weiss, Masters of the Universe Go to Camp: Inside the Bohemian Grove. *Spy Magazine*, November 1989. Retrieved on June 29, 2009.

[21] AmericanHeritage.com, June/July 1980. Richard Reinhardt, *The Bohemian Club.* Retrieved on June 29, 2009.

[22] Garnett, 1908, p. 46.

[23] Garnett, 1908, p. 52.

[24] Garnett, 1908, p. 59.

[25] Garnett, 1908, p. 67.

[26] Garnett, 1908, p. 73.

[27] Garnett, 1908, p. 78.

[28] Scheffauer, Herman George; Arthur Weiss; Bohemian Club. *The Sons of Baldur*, Bohemian Club, 1908.

[29] Bohemian Club. *The grove plays of the Bohemian Club, Volume II.* (1918), Retrieved June 27, 2009.

[30] Bohemian Club. *The grove plays of the Bohemian Club* (1918), Retrieved June 27, 2009.

[31] Internet Archive. *Nec-natama* (Comradeship), a forest play (1914) Retrieved on June 27, 2009.

[32] Wilson, Harry Leon; Domenico Brescia; Bohemian Club. *Life*, Bohemian Club, 1919.

[33] Dobie, Charles Caldwell; Bohemian Club. *Ilya of Murom.* (1920), Retrieved June 27, 2009.

[34] Greene, Clay Meredith; Humphrey John Stewart; Bohemian Club. *St. John of Nepomuk*, The Nineteenth Grove Play, July 30, 1921.

[35] Bohemian Club. *The Rout of the Philistines, A Forest Play* (1922), Retrieved June 27, 2009.

[36] Purrington, Benjamin Allen; Charles Hart; Bohemian Club. *Saul*, 1940.

[37] Pichel, Irving; Charles Hart; Bohemian Club. *Saint Francis of Assisi*, 1927

[38] Young, Waldemar; Edward Harris; Bohemian Club. *Birds of Rhiannon*, A Grove Play, performed Saturday night August 2, 1930.

[39] Dobie, Charles Caldwell; Alec Templeton; Bohemian Club. *The Golden Talisman*, A Grove Play. 1941.

[40] Buck, Richard P.; Bethards, Jack M. (2005). *Music and Musicians in Bohemia: The First One Hundred Years: a Research Document.* The Bohemian Club.

[41] Case, Alexander T.; Ulderico Marcelli; Bohemian Club. *Don Quijote, an Adventure of that Ingenious Gentlemen of La Mancha*, performed July 30, 1955

[42] Totheroh, Dan; Charles Hart; Bohemian Club. *Rip Van Winkle*, the Fifty-fifth Grove Play, 1960

[43] Tourtillot, True; Robert England; Alexander S. McDill. *Agincourt*, the Fifty-seventh Grove Play. 1962

[44] Harline, Leigh; Alexander T. Case; Thomas J. Tyrrell; Bohemian Club. *Sancho Panza*, the Sixtieth Grove Play. 1965

[45] Hackett, Raymond W.; Ralph Moody; Bohemian Club. *The Valley of the Moon*, the Sixty-first Grove Play. 1966

[46] Harline, Leigh; Neill Compton Wilson; Thomas J. Tyrell (director); Lawrence J. Rehag (illustrations); Bohemian Club. *St. John of Bohemia*, the sixty-fourth Grove play of the Bohemian Club as performed by its members in the Bohemian Grove, July 26, 1969.

[47] Magee, David Bickersteth; George Shearing; Bohemian Club. *The Bonny Cravat*, the Sixty-fifth Play of the Bohemian Club Presented at the Grove, July 31, 1970.

[48] Wood, Dale; John Brent Mills; Bohemian Club. *Armada*, the Sixty-ninth Grove Play of the Bohemian Club, Presented July 26, 1974.

[49] Parker, Will A.; Carl J. Eberhard; Peter R. Arnott; Bohemian Club. *Allegory: An Odyssey in Time and Space*, the seventieth Grove Play of the Bohemian Club presented to its members in the Bohemian Grove July 25, 1975.

[50] Pichel, Irving; Charles Hart; Andrew Hoyem; Jay M. Jacobus; Bohemian Club. *Saint Francis of Assisi*, 1982

[51] Archive.org. Regional Oral History Office University of California. William W. Schwarzer, *Litigator, federal district judge, director of the Federal Judicial Center, and professor, 1952-1997 : oral history transcript / 1998*. Retrieved on July 2, 2009.

[52] Blauer, John M.; David A. Bowman; Rod McManigal; Thomas J Tyrrell; Bohemian Club. *Pompeii*, the Eighty-fourth Grove Play, presented July 28, 1989.

[53] McCandless, E. R. "Mac" ; Kenneth B. Baggott; Jay M. Jacobus; Bohemian Club. *The Leonardo Betrayal*, the eighty-ninth Grove Play presented on Friday, July 29, 1994.

[54] McManigal, Rod; Jack Rogers; Thomas J. Tyrrell; Bohemian Club. *Marco Polo*, The ninetieth Grove Play presented Friday, July 28, 1995.

[55] Evans, Richard B.; Ervin, Howard Guy; Devine, Peter Merle; Stegmiller, Kenneth Lawrence. *Casanova*, The Bohemian Club, 2011. Volume 106 of Grove Play.

Bibliography

- Bohemian Club. *History, officers and committees, incorporation, constitution, by-laws and rules, former officers, members, in memoriam*, 1960

- Bohemian Club. *History, officers and committees, incorporation, constitution, by-laws and rules, former officers, members, in memoriam*, 1962

- Domhoff, G. William. *Bohemian Grove and Other Retreats: A Study in Ruling-Class Cohesiveness*, Harper & Row, 1975. ISBN 0-06-131880-9

- Garnett, Porter, *The Bohemian Jinks: A Treatise*, 1908

- Ogden, Dunbar H.; Douglas McDermott; Robert Károly Sarlós (1990). *Theatre West: Image and Impact*. Rodopi. ISBN 90-5183-125-0.

- Scheffauer, Herman George; Arthur Weiss; Bohemian Club. *The Sons of Baldur*, Bohemian Club, 1908.

- Stephens, Henry Morse; Wallace Arthur Sabin, Charles Caldwell Dobie, Bohemian Club. *St. Patrick at Tara*, 1909 Grove play

- Wilson, Harry Leon; Domenico Brescia; Bohemian Club. *Life*, Bohemian Club, 1919.

Chapter 2

Related Bohemian Grove Articles

2.1 Alex Jones (radio host)

For other people named Alex Jones, see Alex Jones (disambiguation).

Alexander Emerick "Alex" Jones (born February 11, 1974) is an American conspiracy theorist,[1][2] radio show host, documentary filmmaker, and writer.[3] His syndicated news/talk show *The Alex Jones Show*, based in Austin, Texas, airs via the Genesis Communications Network[4] and shortwave station WWCR[5] across the United States, and on the Internet in video form.[6][7]

Jones has been the center of many controversies, including his controversial statements about gun control in the wake of the Sandy Hook Elementary School shooting.[8] He has accused the US government of being involved in the Oklahoma City bombing,[9] the September 11 attacks[10] and the filming of fake Moon landings to hide NASA's secret technology.[11][12][13] He believes that government and big business have colluded to create a New World Order through "manufactured economic crises, sophisticated surveillance tech and—above all—inside-job terror attacks that fuel exploitable hysteria".[14] Jones describes himself as a libertarian, paleoconservative and an "aggressive constitutionalist".[15][16]

New York magazine described Jones as "America's leading conspiracy theorist",[17] and the Southern Poverty Law Center describes him as "the most prolific conspiracy theorist in contemporary America."[18] When asked about these labels, Jones said that he finds himself "proud to be listed as a thought criminal against Big Brother".[17]

2.1.1 Early life

Jones was born on February 11, 1974 in Dallas, Texas,[19] and grew up in the Dallas suburb of Rockwall and the city of Austin, Texas. His father David Jones is a dentist and his mother a homemaker.[9] In his video podcasts, he reports that he is of Irish,[20] German, Welsh, mostly[21] British,

and partially Native American descent.[21] He was a lineman on his high school's football team and graduated from Anderson High School in Austin, Texas in 1993.[9] As a teenager, he read Gary Allen's *None Dare Call It Conspiracy*, which strongly impacted him, and which he calls "the easiest-to-read primer on The New World Order".[22] After high school, Jones attended Austin Community College.[23]

2.1.2 Career

Jones began his career in Austin with a live, call-in format public-access television cable TV program. In 1996, Jones switched format to KJFK, hosting a show named *The Final Edition*.[24] During this time Ron Paul was running for Congress and was a guest on Jones's show several times.[25] The two share many beliefs and have been friends since then.[25] In his early shows, he frequently talked about his belief that the US government was behind the Oklahoma City bombing in 1995,[26] using the incident to put down a growing "states rights movement".[27] In 1998, he released his first film, *America Destroyed By Design*.

In 1998, Jones organized a successful effort to build a new Branch Davidian church, as a memorial to those who died during the 1993 fire that ended the government's siege of the original Branch Davidian complex near Waco, Texas.[28] He often featured the project on his public-access television program and claimed that David Koresh and his followers were peaceful people who were murdered by Attorney General Janet Reno and the ATF during the siege.[24]

In 1999, he tied with Shannon Burke for that year's "Best Austin Talk Radio Host" poll as voted by *The Austin Chronicle* readers.[29] Later that year, he was fired from KJFK-FM for refusing to broaden his topics, his viewpoints making the show hard to sell to advertisers, according to the station's operations manager.[24] Jones stated: "It was purely political, and it came down from on high ... I was told 11 weeks ago to lay off Clinton, to lay off all these politicians, to not talk about rebuilding the church, to stop bashing the Marines, A to Z".[24] He began spreading his show via internet connection from his home.[26]

In early 2000, Jones was one of seven Republican candidates for state representative in Texas House District 48, an open seat swing district based in Austin, Texas. Jones stated that he was running "to be a watchdog on the inside",[30] but withdrew from the race after a couple of weeks.

In July, a group of Austin Community Access Center (ACAC) programmers claimed that Jones used legal proceedings and ACAC policy to intimidate them or get their shows thrown off the air.[31]

In 2001, his show was syndicated on approximately 100 stations.[26] After the 9/11 terrorist attack, Jones began to speak of a conspiracy by the Bush administration as being behind the attack, which caused a number of the stations that had previously carried him to drop his program, according to Will Bunch.[32]

On June 8, 2006, while on his way to cover a meeting of the Bilderberg group in Ottawa, Jones was stopped and detained at the Ottawa airport by Canadian authorities who confiscated his passport, camera equipment and most of his belongings. He was later allowed to enter Canada lawfully. Jones said regarding the reason for his immigration hold: "I want to say, on the record, it takes two to tango. I could have handled it better."[33]

On September 8, 2007, he was arrested while protesting at 6th Avenue and 48th Street in New York City. He was charged with operating a bullhorn without a permit. Two others were also cited for disorderly conduct when his group crashed a live television show featuring Geraldo Rivera. In an article one of Jones's fellow protesters said, "It was ... guerrilla information warfare."[34]

2.1.3   Media

Main article: The Alex Jones Show

The Alex Jones Show syndicated radio program is broadcast nationally by the Genesis Communications Network to more than ninety AM and FM radio stations in the United States,[4] and to WWCR Radio shortwave. Live broadcast times are weekdays from 11:00 a.m. to 2:00 p.m. CST and Sundays from 4:00 p.m. to 6:00 p.m. CST. The Sunday broadcast is also broadcast by Emmis Communications' KLBJ Radio.

According to Texas Monthly editor Nate Blakeslee the show had a listenership of 2 million per week in 2010.[35]

According to journalist Will Bunch, a senior fellow at Media Matters for America,[36][37] the show has a demographic heavier in younger viewers than other conservative pundits due to Jones's "highly conspiratorial tone and Web-

oriented approach". Bunch has also stated that "there was always a cast of bottom-feeders like cult radio personality Alex Jones to feed on the deepest paranoia".[32] According to Alexander Zaitchik of Rolling Stone Magazine, in 2011 he had a larger on-line audience than Glenn Beck and Rush Limbaugh combined.[38]

Jones is the operator of several websites centered on news and information about civil liberties issues, global government and a wide variety of current events topics.

2.1.4   Point of view

Jones during a 9/11 Truth Movement event on September 11, 2007, in Manhattan

Political

Mainstream sources have described Jones as a conservative,[39][40][41][42] a right-wing conspiracy theorist,[43][44][45][46] and a libertarian.[47] Jones sees himself as a libertarian and rejects being described as a right-winger.[48] He has also called himself a libertarian,[49] paleoconservative,[50] and an "aggressive constitutionalist".[15][16]

Religious

Jones is a Christian and expresses high regard for the Bible, often citing the more prophetic books of the Bible in order to back up his conspiracy theories,[51] stating: "I just want to try to be a pure and virtuous person. I want to try to transcend my flesh and be the true leader that we're all meant to be... I feel the spirit of the Creator and it embraces me with chills..."[52]

However, he views organized religion as part of the New World Order, saying, "One of the biggest problems in the United States is organized religion. Not just Christians, but Hindus, Muslims, other people. The leaders of their denominations have been funded openly by governments and corporations to preach doctrines of submission to government, submission to tyranny."[53] He is also very critical of Pope Francis, whom he considers to be a socialist advocate of a global government, and a global religion, while ignoring traditional Catholic issues such as abortion.[54]

2.1.5 Controversies

Jones has been the center of many controversies, such as the controversy surrounding his actions and statements about gun control after the Sandy Hook Elementary School shooting.[8] He has accused the US government of being involved in the Oklahoma City bombing[9] and the September 11 attacks.[10] Jones was in a "media crossfire" in 2011, which included criticism by Rush Limbaugh, when the news spread that Jared Lee Loughner, perpetrator of the 2011 Tucson shooting, had been "a fan" of the 9/11 conspiracy film *Loose Change*, of which Jones had been an executive producer.[38]

TV shows and interviews

In January 2013, Jones was invited to speak on Piers Morgan's show after promoting an online petition to deport Morgan due to his support of gun control laws.[55] The interview turned into "a one-person shoutfest, as Jones riffed about guns, oppressive government, the flag, his ancestors' role in Texan independence, and what flag Morgan would have on his tights if they wrestled".[55] The event drew widespread coverage,[55] and according to *The Huffington Post*, Morgan and others such as Glenn Beck "agreed that Jones was a terrible spokesman for gun rights".[56] Jones's appearance on the show was a top trending Twitter topic the following morning.[57]

On June 9, 2013, Jones appeared as a guest on the BBC's television show *Sunday Politics*. During a discussion about conspiracy theories surrounding the Bilderberg Group meetings with presenter Andrew Neil and journalist David Aaronovitch, a critic of such theories, Aaronovitch implied that they either don't exist or Jones is a part of them himself. This was then followed by Jones's shouting and regular interruptions, to which Andrew Neil ended the interview, describing Jones as "an idiot"[58] and "the worst person I've ever interviewed".[59][60] According to Neil on

Twitter, Jones was still shouting until he knew he was off-air.[58][59]

2.1.6 Films

Alex Jones and fans at the Première of A Scanner Darkly, *a film by Richard Linklater, in which Jones has a cameo.*[26]

Author

Film subject

Acting

2.1.7 See also

• 9/11 conspiracy theories

2.1.8 References

[1] Byford, Jovan (2011-10-12). *Conspiracy Theories: A Critical Introduction*. Palgrave Macmillan. p. 11. ISBN 9780230349216. Retrieved 23 November 2013.

[2] Alex Seitz-Wald. "Alex Jones: Boston explosion a government conspiracy". *salon.com*.

[3] "Glenn Beck's Shtick? Alex Jones Got There First". *Rolling Stone*.

[4] List of Alex Jones Radio Show Affiliated Stations.

[5] "WWCR.com - Home - WWCR Shortwave, Nashville, Tennessee, USA". *wwcr.com*.

[6] "All Hell Breaks Loose on The View After 9/11 Truther Cuts Loose". *FoxNation.com*.

[7] "The Alex Jones Show". Tune In. Retrieved January 13, 2013.

[8] "Alex Jones' pro-gun tirade at Piers Morgan on British presenter's own show". *The Guardian* (London). January 8, 2013. Retrieved January 10, 2013.

[9] Zaitchik, Alexander (2011-03-02). "Meet Alex Jones, the Talk Radio Host Behind Charlie Sheen's Crazy Rants". *Rolling Stone*. Archived from the original on March 29, 2011. Retrieved 2011-03-24.

[10] Stahl, Jeremy (September 6, 2011). "Where Did 9/11 Conspiracies Come From?". *Slate*. Retrieved September 11, 2011.

[11] Nuzzi, Olivia. "Dear Moon Landing Deniers: Sorry I Called You Moon Landing Deniers". The Daily Beast. Retrieved 27 August 2014.

[12] "Moon Landing Faked!!!—Why People Believe in Conspiracy Theories". April 30, 2013. Retrieved 4 August 2015.

[13] Zara, Christopher (June 9, 2013). "Alex Jones Blows Up On BBC Sunday Politics For Bilderberg Group Follow-Up: If My Enemies Murder Me, It Makes Me A Martyr". International Business Times. Retrieved 31 August 2014.

[14] Alexander Zaitchik (March 2, 2011). "Meet Alex Jones". *Rolling Stone*. Retrieved February 24, 2013.

[15] "The Alex Jones Show". Austin, TX: KLBJ. July 21, 2008. Archived from the original on September 26, 2010.

[16] Hammack, Laurence (June 6, 2009). "Roanoke man charged with making online threats". *The Roanoke Times*. Archived from the original on June 9, 2009.

[17] Ciscarelli, Joe. "An Interview With Alex Jones, America's Leading (and Proudest) Conspiracy Theorist". Retrieved 8 September 2014.

[18] "Alex Jones Profile". Southern Poverty Law Center.

[19] Jones, Alex. *Coast to Coast AM*. January 27, 2007.

[20] The Alex Jones Channel (April 29, 2015). "Baltimore City Councilman Pushes Racial Division". *YouTube*. Google. Retrieved April 30, 2015.

[21] *Alex Jones Puts Anti-Semitic Caller in His Place!!* (2011-03-04). Alex Jones Channel/Prisonplanet.tv/Genesis Communications Network. Retrieved April 06, 2014.

[22] "Meet Alex Jones". *Rolling Stone*. Retrieved January 10, 2013.

[23] Howard Stern Radio Show, February 26, 2013.

[24] Nichols, Lee (December 10, 1999). "Psst, It's a Conspiracy: KJFK Gives Alex Jones the Boot Media Clips". The Austin Chronicle.

[25] "How Radio Host Alex Jones Has Cornered the Bipartisan Paranoia Market". *New York*. Retrieved January 11, 2013.

[26] "Meet Alex Jones". *Rolling Stone*. Retrieved January 10, 2013.

[27] Kay, Jonathan (2011-05-17). *Among the Truthers: A Journey Through America's Growing Conspiracist Underground*. HarperCollins. pp. 26–. ISBN 9780062004819. Retrieved January 11, 2013.

[28] Connie Mabin (April 19, 2000). "Branch Davidians hope a new church can close wounds". *The Independent* (UK). Associated Press. Retrieved January 29, 2011.

[29] "Best of Austin 1999 Readers Poll". 1999. Retrieved 2007-08-14.

[30] Scott S. Greenberger (January 4, 2000). "Nine to seek Greenberg's House seat" (fee required). *Austin American-Statesman*. p. B1.

[31] Nichols, Lee (2000-07-14). "Alex Jones: Conspiracy Victim or Evil Mastermind?". *The Austin Chronicle*. Archived from the original on 2012-01-02. Retrieved 2008-05-20. Alex Jones is no stranger to conspiracy theories.

[32] Bunch, Will (2011-09-13). *The Backlash: Right-Wing Radicals, High-Def Hucksters, and Paranoid Politics in the Age of Obama*. HarperCollins. pp. 73–. ISBN 9780061991721. Retrieved January 10, 2013.

[33] Payton, Laura (2006-06-08). "Bilderberg-bound filmmaker held at airport". *Ottawa Citizen*. Retrieved 2007-08-13.

[34] Grace, Melissa; Xana O'Neill (2007-09-09). "Filmmaker arrested during city protest". *Daily News (New York)*. Archived from the original on 13 October 2007. Retrieved 2007-09-10.

[35] Blakeslee, Nate (March 2010). "Alex Jones Is About To Explode". Texas Monthly. Retrieved 29 August 2014.

[36] "Will Bunch". CommonDreams. Retrieved 29 August 2014.

[37] "Will Bunch". The Huffington Post. Retrieved 29 August 2014.

[38] ALEXANDER ZAITCHIK (March 2, 2011). "Meet Alex Jones". *Rolling Stone*. Retrieved January 10, 2013.

[39] "BART Officer Threats". cbs5.com. Retrieved 2010-12-13.

[40] An article in the *San Jose Mercury News* describes Alex Jones as a "conservative radio talk show host".

[41] Two articles in the *St. Louis Post-Dispatch* from March and April 2009 describe Jones as a "conservative radio commentator"

[42] Norman, Tony (2009-08-14). "A nutty way of discussing health care". *Pittsburgh Post-Gazette*.

[43] Gosa, Travis L. (2011). "Counterknowledge, racial paranoia, and the cultic milieu: Decoding hip hop conspiracy theory". *Poetics* **39** (3): 187. doi:10.1016/j.poetic.2011.03.003. Retrieved 2011-07-11.

[44] Black, Louis (2000-07-14). "Unknown Title". *Austin Chronicle*. Retrieved 2008-05-20. Jones is an articulate, sometimes hypnotic, often just annoying conspiracy theorist.

[45] Duggan, Paul (2001-10-26). "Austin Hears the Music And Another New Reality; In Texas Cultural Center, People Prepare to Fight Terror" (Fee required). *Washington Post*. p. A22. Retrieved 2008-05-20. [His cable show] has made the exuberant, 27-year-old conspiracy theorist a minor celebrity in Austin.

[46] "Conspiracy Files: 9/11 - Q&A: What really happened" (FAQ). BBC News. 2007-02-16. Retrieved 2008-05-19. Leading conspiracy theorist and broadcaster Alex Jones of *infowars.com* argues that ...

[47] ABC News. "The Return of Alex Jones". *ABC News*.

[48] Roddy, Dennis B. (April 10, 2009). "An Accused Cop Killer's Politics". *Slate*. Retrieved July 23, 2009.

[49] Rosell, Rich (27 November 2006). "Dark days, the Alex Jones interview". *digitallyobsessed.com*.

[50] Rosell, Rich (27 November 2006). "digitallyobsessed.com.". *Dark days, the Alex Jones interview*.

[51] "The religion and political views of Alex Jones". Retrieved December 24, 2014.

[52] "Alex Jones Tv 1/2: Alex Takes Your Calls on Religion". Retrieved December 24, 2014.

[53] "Alex Jones on organized religion and resistance". Retrieved December 24, 2014.

[54] "» Special Report: Pope Francis Is A Vatican Coup Alex Jones' Infowars: There's a war on for your mind!". *Infowars*.

[55] "Piers Morgan vs. Alex Jones feud: helping or hurting gun control? (+video)". *The Christian Science Monitor*. Retrieved January 10, 2013.

[56] Mirkinson, Jack (January 9, 2013). "Piers Morgan: Alex Jones 'Terrifying', A Perfect 'Advertisement For Gun Control'". *The Huffington Post*. Retrieved January 9, 2013.

[57] "Social media abuzz over Piers Morgan vs. Alex Jones". *CNN*. Retrieved January 10, 2013.

[58] Dixon, Hayley (June 9, 2013). "'Idiot' Bilderberg conspiracy theorist Alex Jones disrupts BBC politics show". *telegraph.co.uk* (London). Retrieved June 9, 2013.

[59] Topping, Alexandra (June 9, 2013). "Andrew Neil calls Alex Jones an idiot in Sunday Politics clash". *guardian.co.uk* (London). Retrieved June 9, 2013.

[60] Taylor, Adam (9 June 2013). "Conspiracy Theorist Alex Jones Goes Berserk During BBC Show". *Business Insider*. Retrieved 9 June 2013.

2.1.9 External links

- Alex Jones at the Internet Movie Database

2.2 Belizean Grove

Belizean Grove logo

The **Belizean Grove** is an elite, invitation-only American women's social club, located at 17 East 89th Street in New York City.[1][2] Founded in 1999 by Susan Stautberg, a former Westinghouse Broadcasting executive, and Edie Weiner, a futurist,[3] the Belizean Grove includes approximately 115 to 125 influential members from the military, financial, and diplomatic sectors. It is the female equivalent to the male-only social group, the Bohemian Club, whose annual meetings are held at the Bohemian Grove in California.[2] The Belizean Grove meets annually in Belize or similar Central American locations.[4] They also meet in New York and other U.S. cities, for activities they describe as "a balance of fun, substantive programs and bonding".[5]

Notable members of the Belizean Grove include former General Services Administration Administrator Lurita Doan and U.S. Army General Ann E. Dunwoody.[2][6] High-level executives from Goldman Sachs, Victoria's Secret, and Harley-Davidson also belong to the Grove, as do some ambassadors.[5] Other business leaders include: Davia Temin,[7] CEO and Founder of Temin and Company, Catherina Allen, CEO of Santa Fe Group,[8] and Ann Kaplan of Circle Financial Group.[9] Supreme Court justice Sonia Sotomayor was a member of the Grove until June 19, 2009, when she resigned after Republican senators voiced concerns over the group's women-only membership policy.[10][11][12][13]

2.2.1 See also

- Gentlemen's club

- Women's club

2.2.2 References

[1] Gutner, Toddi (2001-02-19). "Move Over, Bohemian Grove". *BusinessWeek*. Archived from the original on 12 June 2009. Retrieved 2009-06-05.

[2] Vogel, Kenneth P. (2009-06-04). "Sonia Sotomayor found friends in elite group". *The Politico*. Archived from the original on 8 June 2009. Retrieved 2009-06-05.

[3] http://weineredrichbrown.com/our-team/edie-weiner-bio/

[4] http://technorati.com/women/article/the-belizean-grove-old-girls-club/

[5] Savage, Charlie and Kirkpatrick, David D. (2009-06-15). "Sotomayor Defends Ties to Association". *The New York Times*. Archived from the original on 20 June 2009. Retrieved 2009-06-16.

[6] Cohen, Andrew (2009-06-05). "Is Sotomayor Supremely Stylish?". *Vanity Fair*. Archived from the original on 9 June 2009. Retrieved 2009-06-05.

[7] Davia Temin

[8] http://www.folkartmarket.org/news/members-of-the-professional-womens-club-belizean-grove-tdline-analysts-from-the-mkey

[9] Ryckman, Pamela (2011-04-02). "Belizean Grove, a Mighty Women's Club, Keeps a Low Profile". *The New York Times*.

[10] Sherman, Mark (2009-06-19). "Sotomayor Quits Belizean Grove". *Huffington Post*. Associated Press. Archived from the original on 20 June 2009. Retrieved 2009-06-19.

[11] Bravin, Jess (2009-06-20). "Court Nominee Sotomayor Quits Women-Only Group". *The Wall Street Journal*. Archived from the original on 23 June 2009. Retrieved 2009-06-20.

[12] "Sotomayor resigns from women's club". CNN. 2009-06-19. Archived from the original on 24 June 2009. Retrieved 2009-06-20.

[13] Cooper, Helene (2009-06-20). "Sotomayor quits club". *The Seattle Times*. Archived from the original on 21 June 2009. Retrieved 2009-06-20.

2.3 Elizabeth Crocker Bowers

Elizabeth Crocker Bowers (March 12, 1830 – November 6, 1895) [1] was an American stage actress and theatrical manager.[2][3] She was also known professionally as **Mrs. D. P. Bowers**.

2.3.1 Early life

Elizabeth Crocker Bowers was born March 12, 1830 in Stamford, Connecticut,[4] the daughter of an Episcopal clergyman[1] and sister of actress Sarah Crocker Conway (also known as Mrs. F. B. Conway).[4]

2.3.2 Career and marriages

In 1846, she appeared in the character of Amanthis [1] at the Park Theatre in New York City, New York.[3]

On March 4, 1847,[1][4] she married actor David P. Bowers,[3] and moved to Philadelphia. She appeared as Donna Victoria in *A Bold Stroke for a Husband* at the Walnut Street Theatre in Philadelphia. She became very popular at the Arch Street Theatre, and made Philadelphia her home until her husband's death in 1857.[4]

In December 1857, after a period of retirement from the stage, she leased the Walnut Street Theatre and retained its management until 1859. She then leased the Philadelphia Academy of Music for a short dramatic season.[1]

She married Dr. Brown of Baltimore in 1861.[3] and traveled to London. She made a great success as "Julia" in *The Hunchback* at the Sadler's Wells Theatre and "Geraldine D'Arcy" in *Woman (play)* at the Lyceum Theatre in London.[3]

Returning to New York City in 1863, she played for a time at the Winter Garden (now demolished). Among her favorite roles were Juliet, Lady Macbeth, Marie Antoinette, and Lady Audley.[3]

After the death of Dr. Brown in 1867, she married actor J. C. McCollom,[4] with whom she repeated many of her popular roles.[3]

Her subsequent retirement in Philadelphia was interrupted by a return to the stage in October 1886 for several years.[3] She organized a new dramatic company, and visited the principal cities of the U.S., playing many of her old and favorite characters. Under A. M. Palmer's management she appeared in *Lady Windermere's Fan* (1893), and later she was a supporting actress for Rose Coghlan and Olga Nethersole.[1]

Bowers died of pneumonia and heart failure [4] on November 6, 1895[3] in at the home of her son-in-law, Frank Bennett, in Washington D.C. She was survived by a daughter, Mrs. F. V.(May) Bennett and two sons, Harry C. Bowers of Portland, OR and Walter Bowers of New York City.[5] She was buried at Rock Creek Cemetery in Washington, D.C.[6]

2.3.3 References

[1] "Bowers,_Elizabeth_Crocker". *Appletons' Cyclopædia of American Biography* (revised ed.). 1900. Retrieved January 29, 2013.

[2] Barnhart, Clarence L., ed. (1954). "Bowers, Elizabeth Crocker". *New Century Cyclopedia of Names, Volume One, A – Emin Pasha*. New York: Appleton-Century-Crofts. p. 607.

[3] Gilman, Daniel Coit (1905). *The New International Encyclopedia*. New York: Dodd, Mead. p. 381.

[4] "Mrs. D. P. Bowers, A Footlight Favorite, Passes Quietly Away". *The Norfolk Virginian*. November 7, 1895. Retrieved January 29, 2013.

[5] "Mrs. D. P. Bowers Dead". *The San Francisco Call*. November 7, 1895. Retrieved January 29, 2013.

[6] "Famous Actress is Dead". *The Morning Times (Washington, D. C.)*. November 7, 1895. Retrieved January 29, 2013.

2.3.4 External links

- Elizabeth Crocker Bowers; *North American Theatre Online*(AlexanderStreet)

- portrait with sister Sarah Crocker Conway(AlexanderStreet)

2.4 George Sterling

For the Canadian politician, see George A. Sterling.

George Sterling (December 1, 1869 – November 17,

George Sterling shortly before his death in 1926[1]

1926) was an American poet and playwright based in California who, during his time, was celebrated in Northern California as one of the greatest American poets, although he never gained much fame in the rest of the United States.

2.4.1 Biography

Sterling was born in Sag Harbor, Long Island, New York, the eldest of nine children. His father was Dr. George A. Sterling, a physician who determined to make a priest of one of his sons, and George was selected to attend, for three years, St. Charles College in Maryland. He was instructed in English by poet John B. Tabb. His mother Mary was a member of the Havens family, prominent in Sag Harbor and the Shelter Island area. Her brother, Frank C. Havens, Sterling's uncle, went to San Francisco in the late 19th century and established himself as a prominent lawyer and real estate developer. Sterling eventually followed him to the Bay Area in 1890 and worked for eighteen years as a real estate broker.

Sterling became a significant figure in Bohemian literary circles in northern California in the first quarter of the 20th century, and in the development of the artists' colony in Carmel. He was mentored by a much older Ambrose Bierce, and became close friends with Jack London and Clark Ashton Smith, and later mentor to Robinson Jeffers. His association with Charles Rollo Peters may have led to his move to Carmel. The hamlet had been discovered by Charles Warren Stoddard and others, but Sterling made it world famous. His aunt Missus Havens purchased a home for him in Carmel Pines where he lived for six years.

Kevin Starr (1973) wrote:

> "The uncrowned King of Bohemia (so his friends called him), Sterling had been at the center of every artistic circle in the San Francisco Bay Area. Celebrated as the embodiment of the local artistic scene, though forgotten today, Sterling had in his lifetime been linked with the immortals, his name carved on the walls of the Panama-Pacific International Exposition next to the great poets of the past."

Joseph Noel (1940) says that Sterling's poem, *A Wine of Wizardry*,[2] has "been classed by many authorities as the greatest poem ever written by an American author."

According to Noel, Sterling sent the final draft of *A Wine of Wizardry* to the normally acerbic and critical Ambrose Bierce. Bierce said "If I could find a flaw in it, I should quickly call your attention to it... It takes the breath away."

Sterling joined the Bohemian Club and acted in their theatrical productions each summer at the Bohemian Grove.[3]

Sterling, posing with caricatures of himself at the Bohemian Grove,
1907

George Sterling posed for an illustration by Adelaide Hanscom
Leeson which appeared in a printing of the Rubaiyat of Omar
Khayyam.

For the main Grove play in 1907, the club presented *The Triumph of Bohemia*, Sterling's verse drama depicting the battle between the "Spirit of Bohemia" and Mammon for the souls of the grove's woodmen.[4] Sterling also supplied lyric for the musical numbers at the 1918 Grove play.[3]

Bierce, who acclaimed Sterling's poem *The Testimony of the Suns*, in his "Prattle" column in William Randolph Hearst's *San Francisco Examiner*, arranged for the publication of *A Wine of Wizardry* in the September 1907 number of *Cosmopolitan*, which afforded Sterling some national notice. In an introduction to the poem, Bierce wrote "Whatever length of days may be according to this magazine, it is not likely to do anything more notable in literature than it accomplished in this issue by the publication of Mr. George Sterling's poem, 'A Wine of Wizardry.'" Bierce wrote to Sterling, "I hardly know how to speak of it. No poem in English of equal length has so bewildering a wealth of imagination. Not Spencer himself has flung such a profusion of jewels into so small a casket".

Sterling fell into drinking and his wife departed. Noel, a personal acquaintance, says that when he began the poem, Sterling "was persuaded that there was another world than that we know. He repeated this to me so frequently that it became a trifle tiresome. Of the means he employed to

get a glimpse of that other world, I am not so sure." He observes that "many before Sterling had used narcotics to this end;" that "George, a doctor's son, had always had access to whatever drugs he fancied;" says that Sterling's wife said "that George had purloined a great quantity of opium from his brother Wickham," and speaks of "internal evidence in the poem" in which "Sterling writes his Fancy awakened with a 'brow caressed by poppybloom.'" Despite all this, Noel makes a point of saying "there is no direct evidence that Sterling used narcotics."

Sterling also wrote for children, *The Saga of the Pony Express*.

Despite such famous mentors as Bierce and Ina Coolbrith, and his long association with London, Sterling himself never became well known outside California.

Sterling's poetry is both visionary and mystical, but he also wrote ribald quatrains that were often unprintable and left unpublished. His style reflects the Romantic charm of such poets as Shelley, Keats and Poe, and he provided guidance and encouragement to the similarly-inclined Clark Ashton Smith at the beginning of Smith's own career.

Sterling carried a vial of cyanide for many years. When asked about it he said "A prison becomes a home if you have the key".[5] Finally in November 1926, Sterling used it at his residence at the San Francisco Bohemian Club. Kevin Starr wrote that "When George Sterling's corpse was discovered in his room at the Bohemian Club... the golden age of San Francisco's bohemia had definitely come to a miserable end."

Sterling's most famous line was delivered to the city of San Francisco, "the cool, grey city of love!".[6]

2.4.2 Trivia

- Sterling Road in Berkeley is named for George Sterling.

- A stone bench was dedicated to Sterling on June 25, 1926 at the crest of Hyde Street on Russian Hill.

- He is depicted twice in Jack London's novels: as Russ Brissenden in the autobiographical *Martin Eden* (1909) and as Mark Hall in *The Valley of the Moon* (1913).

2.4.3 Selected works

Poetry volumes

- *The Testimony of the Suns and Other Poems* (San Francisco: W. E. Wood, 1903; San Francisco: A. M. Robertson, 1904, 1907)

- *A Wine of Wizardry and Other Poems* (San Francisco: A. M. Robertson, 1909).

- *The House of Orchids and Other Poems* (San Francisco: A. M. Robertson, 1911).

- *Beyond the Breakers and Other Poems* (San Francisco: A. M. Robertson, 1914).

- *Ode on the Opening of the Panama-Pacific International Exposition* (San Francisco: A. M. Robertson, 1915).

- *The Evanescent City* (San Francisco: A. M. Robertson, 1915).

- *The Caged Eagle and Other Poems* (San Francisco: A. M. Robertson, 1916).

- *Yosemite: An Ode* (San Francisco: A. M. Robertson, 1915).

- *The Binding of the Beast and Other War Verse* (San Francisco: A. M. Robertson, 1917).

- *Thirty-Five Sonnets* (San Francisco: Book Club of California, 1917).

- *To a Girl Dancing* (San Francisco: Grabhorn, 1921).

- *Sails and Mirage and Other Poems* (San Francisco: A. M. Robertson, 1921).

- *Selected Poems* (New York: Henry Holt, 1923; San Francisco: A. M. Robertson, 1923).

- *Strange Waters* (San Francisco: Paul Elder [?], 1926).

- *The Testimony of the Suns, Including Comments, Suggestions, and Annotations by Ambrose Bierce: A Facsimile of the Original Typewritten Manuscript* (San Francisco: Book Club of California, 1927).

- *Sonnets to Craig*, Upton Sinclair, ed. (Long Beach, Calif.: Upton Sinclair, 1928; New York: Albert & Charles Boni, 1928).

- *Poems to Vera* (New York: Oxford University Press, 1938).

- *After Sunset*, R. H. Barlow, ed. (San Francisco: John Howell, 1939).

- *A Wine of Wizardry and Three Other Poems*, Dale L. Walker, ed. (Fort Johnson: "a private press," 1964).

- *George Sterling: A Centenary Memoir-Anthology*, Charles Angoff, ed. (South Brunswick and New York: Poetry Society of America, 1969).

- *The Thirst of Satan: Poems of Fantasy and Terror*, S. T. Joshi, ed. (New York: Hippocampus Press, 2003).

- *Complete Poetry*, S. T. Joshi and David E. Schultz, eds. (New York: Hippocampus Press, 2013).

Plays

- *The Triumph of Bohemia: A Forest Play* (San Francisco: Bohemian Club, 1907).

- with Hugo Hofmannsthal: *The Play of Everyman* (San Francisco: A. M. Robertson, 1917; Los Angeles: Primavera Press, 1939).

- *Lilith: A Dramatic Poem* (San Francisco: A. M. Robertson, 1919; San Francisco: Book Club of California, 1920; New York: Macmillan, 1926).

- *Rosamund: A Dramatic Poem* (San Francisco: A. M. Robertson, 1920).

- *Truth* (Chicago: Bookfellows, 1923; San Francisco: Bohemian Club, 1926).

Songs

- with Lawrence Zenda (Rosaliene Travis, pseud.): *Songs* (San Francisco: Sherman, Clay, 1916, 1918, 1928).

- with Lawrence Zenda (Rosaliene Travis, pseud.): *You Are So Beautiful* (San Francisco: Sherman, Clay, 1917).

- *We're A-Going* (San Francisco: Sherman, Clay, 1918).

Prose

- *Robinson Jeffers: The Man and the Artist* (New York: Boni & Liveright, 1926).

Letters

- *Give a Man a Boat He Can Sail: Letters of George Sterling,* James Henry, Ed. (Detroit: Harlo, 1980).

- *From Baltimore to Bohemia: The Letters of H. L. Mencken and George Sterling,* ed. S. T. Joshi (Rutherford, NJ: Fairleigh Dickinson University, 2001).

- *Dear Master: Letters of George Sterling to Ambrose Bierce, 1900-1912,* Roger K. Larson, ed. (San Francisco: Book Club of California; 2002).

- *The Shadow of the Unattained: The Letters of George Sterling and Clark Ashton Smith,* David E. Schultz and S. T. Joshi, eds. (New York: Hippocampus Press, 2005).

Edited volumes

- with Bertha Clark Pope: *Letters of Ambrose Bierce* (San Francisco: Book Club of California, 1922).

  Although uncredited, Sterling was co-editor of this volume.

- with Genevieve Taggard and James Rorty, *Continent's End* (San Francisco: Book Club of California, 1925).

2.4.4   References

Notes

[1] O'Day, Edward F. (December 1927). "1869-1926". *Overland Monthly.* LXXXV (12): 357–359.

[2] A Wine of Wizardry at www.idiom.com

[3] Mencken, Henry Louis; Sterling, George; Joshi, S. T. *From Baltimore to Bohemia: the letters of H.L. Mencken and George Sterling*, Fairleigh Dickinson Univ Press, 2001, p. 252. ISBN 0-8386-3869-4

[4] Weir, David. *Decadent culture in the United States: art and literature against the American grain, 1890-1926*, SUNY Press, 2007, p. 144. ISBN 0-7914-7277-9

[5] The Documentary "The Gospel According to Philip K. Dick"

[6] The Cool, Grey City of Love, by George Sterling at alangullette.com

Bibliography

- Benediktsson, Thomas E. (1980). *George Sterling.* Boston: Twayne Publishers. ISBN 0-8057-7313-4.

- Cusatis, John (2006). "George Sterling." *Greenwood Encyclopedia of American Poets and Poetry,* Volume 5, Westport, CT: Greenwood Publishers, 1530-1531.

- Joshi, S. T. (2008). "George Sterling: Prophet of the Suns," chapter 1 in *Emperors of Dreams: Some Notes on Weird Poetry.* Sydney: P'rea Press. ISBN 978-0-9804625-3-1 (pbk) and ISBN 978-0-9804625-4-8 (hbk).

- Noel, Joseph (1940). *Footloose in Arcadia.* New York: Carrick and Evans.

- Parry, Albert (1933, first edition). "Lovely Chaos in Carmel and Taos", chapter 20 within *Garretts & Pretenders: A History of Bohemianism in America,* republished in 1960 and 2005, Cosimo, Inc. ISBN 1-59605-090-X

- Starr, Kevin (1973). *Americans and the California Dream 1850-1915.* Oxford University Press. 1986 reprint: ISBN 0-19-504233-6

2.4.5   External links

- George-Sterling.org Collected works, image gallery, bibliography and critical articles.

- A George Sterling Page: A brief biography of Sterling.

- George Sterling, Poet: A page by the poet's grand niece.

- George Sterling (1869-1926): A collection of Sterling's poems; notes on memorial glade in San Francisco.

- *George Sterling: Poet and Friend* by Clark Ashton Smith

- 5 short radio episodes from Sterling's poems at California Legacy Project.

- Guide to the Collection of George Sterling Papers at The Bancroft Library

- Free scores by George Sterling at the International Music Score Library Project

- Works by or about George Sterling at Internet Archive

- Works by George Sterling at LibriVox (public domain audiobooks) ◀))

2.5 Haig Patigian

Newspaper clipping of Haig Patigian standing next to his bust of Helen Wills, October 1928

Haig Patigian (Armenian: Հայկ Պաղիկեան; January 22, 1876 – September 19, 1950) was an Armenian-American sculptor

Patigian was born on in the city of Van in the Ottoman Empire. His parents were teachers at the American Mission School in Armenia. He was largely self-taught as a sculptor.Patigian spent most of his career in San Francisco, California and most of his works are located in California. The Oakland Museum in Oakland, California, includes a large number of his works in its collection, and more can be seen in and around San Francisco City Hall.

Patigian was an active member of the Bohemian Club, serving two terms as club president. He designed the Owl Shrine, a 40-foot high hollow concrete and steel structure which was built in the 1920s to have the appearance of a natural rock outcropping which happened to resemble an owl.[1] The Owl Shrine became the centerpiece of the *Cremation of Care* ceremony at the Bohemian Grove in 1929.[2]

Patigian married Blanche Hollister of Courtland, California, in 1908.[3]

2.5.1 Selected public works

Entrance of 600 Stockton, San Francisco, the former Metropolitan Life building, now a Ritz-Carlton hotel. Visible behind a decorated Christmas tree are the Ionic columns surmounted by a pediment containing a tableau created in 1920 by Patigian for his client Timothy L. Pflueger of Miller and Pflueger, architects

- McKinley statue in Arcata, California, 1906

- *Electricity*, *Imagination*, *Invention* and *Steam*; four repeated sculptures at the Machinery Palace, Panama-Pacific International Exposition (1915) (destroyed)[4]

- General John Pershing, San Francisco, California, 1921

- *Abraham Lincoln*, San Francisco, California, 1928

- Thomas Starr King (1931)

  This work resided in the Capitol Building in Washington D.C. as one of California's contributions to the National Statuary Hall Collection

Vanity, shown in 1916 at the Palace of Fine Arts

until being replaced by a statue of Ronald Reagan in 2009.

- *Volunteer Firemen Memorial*, San Francisco, California, 1933

2.5.2   Architectural sculpture

- M. H. de Young Memorial Museum, tympanum, San Francisco, California, circa 1895 (removed)

- San Francisco Savings Union Bank building, pediment, San Francisco, California, 1911

- Palace of Fine Art & the Machinery Palace, (now destroyed) Panama-Pacific Exposition, San Francisco, California, 1915

- Metropolitan Life Insurance Building, (now the Ritz Carlton Hotel) pediment, San Francisco, California, 1920

- *Navigation, Aviation*, and *Industry*, Richfield Tower, Los Angeles, California, allegorical figures, 1928

    when the building was demolished in 1968 the figures were moved to the Art Museum of the University of California, Santa Barbara

- Department of Commerce Building, pediment, Washington D.C., 1934

2.5.3   References

[1] Starr, Kevin (2002). *The Dream Endures: California Enters the 1940s*. Oxford University Press. ISBN 0-19-515797-4.

[2] Cross, Francis L. (1972). *The Annals of the Bohemian Club for the years 1907-1972, Centennial Edition, volume V*. San Francisco: Bohemian Club and Recorder-Sunset Press.

[3] Herringshaw, Thomas William. *American Elite and Sociologist Bluebook*, p. 387. American Blue Book Publishers, 1922.

[4] Todd, Frank Morton (1921). *The Story of the Exposition (Volume Two of Five)*. New York, London: G. P. Putnam's Sons, The Knickerbocker Press.

- Kvaran, Einar Einarsson, Architectural Sculpture in America, unpublished manuscript

- National Sculpture Society, Contemporary American Sculpture 1929, National Sculpture Society, New York, NY 1929

- Opitz, Glenn B, Editor, Mantle Fielding's Dictionary of American Painters, Sculptors & Engravers, Apollo Book, Poughkeepsie NY, 1986

- Proske, Beatrice Gilman, Brookgreen Gardens Sculpture, Brookgreen Gardens, South Carolina, 1968

2.5.4   External links

- Painted portrait of Haig Patigian with Bohemian Owl in background, by Peter Ilyin (1927). Online Archive of California.

2.6   Ina Coolbrith

Ina Donna Coolbrith (March 10, 1841 – February 29, 1928) was an American poet, writer, librarian, and a prominent figure in the San Francisco Bay Area literary community. Called the "Sweet Singer of California",[1] she was the first California Poet Laureate and the first poet laureate of any American state.[2]

Coolbrith, born the niece of Latter Day Saint movement founder Joseph Smith, left the Mormon community as a child to enter her teens in Los Angeles, California, where she began to publish poetry. She terminated a youthful failed marriage to make her home in San Francisco, and met writers Bret Harte and Charles Warren Stoddard with eled by train to New York City several times and, with fewer worldly cares, greatly increased her poetry output. On June 30, 1915, Coolbrith was named California's poet laureate, and she continued to write poetry for eight more years. Her style was more than the usual melancholic or uplifting themes expected of women—she included a wide variety of subjects in her poems, which were noted as being "singularly sympathetic" and "palpably spontaneous".[3] Her sensuous descriptions of natural scenes advanced the art of Victorian poetry to incorporate greater accuracy without trite sentiment, foreshadowing the Imagist school and the work of Robert Frost.[4] California poet laureate Carol Muske-Dukes wrote of Coolbrith's poems that, though they "were steeped in a high tea lavender style", influenced by a British stateliness, "California remained her inspiration."[5]

2.6.1 Early life

Ina Coolbrith in the 1880s

whom she formed the "Golden Gate Trinity" closely associated with the literary journal *Overland Monthly*. Her poetry received positive notice from critics and established poets such as Mark Twain, Ambrose Bierce and Alfred Lord Tennyson. She held literary salons at her home—in this way she introduced new writers to publishers. Coolbrith befriended the poet Joaquin Miller and helped him gain global fame.

While Miller toured Europe and lived out their mutual dream of visiting Lord Byron's tomb, Coolbrith was saddled with custody of his daughter, and the care of members of her own family, so she set up house in Oakland and accepted the position of city librarian. Her poetry suffered as a result of her long work hours, but she mentored a generation of young readers including Jack London and Isadora Duncan. After she served for 19 years, Oakland's library patrons called for reorganization, and Coolbrith was fired. She moved back to San Francisco and was invited by members of the Bohemian Club to be their librarian.

Coolbrith began to write a history of California literature, including much autobiographical material, but the fire following the 1906 San Francisco earthquake consumed her work. Author Gertrude Atherton and Coolbrith's Bohemian Club friends helped set her up again in a new house, and she resumed writing and holding literary salons. She trav-

Coolbrith in her youth

Ina Coolbrith was born **Josephine Donna Smith** in Nauvoo, Illinois, the last of three daughters of Agnes Moulton Coolbrith and Don Carlos Smith, brother to Joseph Smith[6] Coolbrith's father died of malarial fever four months after her birth,[7] and a sister died one month after that;[6] Coolbrith's mother then married Joseph Smith, in 1842, becoming his sixth or seventh wife, depending on whether Fanny Alger is counted as a wife or as a lover.[8]

No children came of the union—Agnes felt neglected in her unfruitful Levirate marriage, the only such marriage of Smith.[9] Over the next two years, Smith married some 20 to 30 more wives, angering non-Mormons in the area. In June 1844, Smith was killed at the hands of an anti-Mormon, anti-polygamist mob. Losing her faith and fearful of her life, Coolbrith's mother left the Latter-day Saint community[10] and moved to Saint Louis, Missouri, where she married a printer and lawyer named William Pickett.[11] Twin sons were born to the couple,[6] and in 1851 Pickett traveled overland with his new family to California in a wagon train. On the long trek, the young Ina read from a book of Shakespeare's works and from a collection of Byron's poems.[1] As a ten-year-old girl, Ina entered California in front of the wagon train with the famous African-American scout Jim Beckwourth, riding with him on his horse, through what would later be named Beckwourth Pass. The family settled in Los Angeles, California,[10] and Pickett established a law practice.[11]

To avoid identification with her former family or with Mormonism, Ina's mother reverted to using her maiden name, Coolbrith. The family resolved not to speak of their Mormon past, and it was only after Ina Coolbrith's death that the public learned of her origin.[12]

Coolbrith, sometimes called "Josephina" or just "Ina", wrote poems beginning at age 11,[13] first publishing "My Ideal Home" in a newspaper in 1856, writing as Ina Donna Coolbrith.[4] Her work appeared in the Poetry Corner of the *Los Angeles Star*, and in the *California Home Journal*. As she grew into young womanhood, Coolbrith was renowned for her beauty; she was selected to open a ball with Pío Pico, the last Mexican governor of California.[14] In April 1858 at the age of 17, she married Robert Bruce Carsley, an iron-worker and part-time actor, but she suffered abuse at his hands,[4] and further emotional pain came from the death of the couple's infant son. An altercation between Pickett and Carsley resulted in a bullet mutilating Carsley's hand, requiring amputation.[6] Carsley accused Coolbrith of infidelity,[15] and she divorced him in a sensational public trial; the dissolution was final on December 30, 1861.[6] Her later poem, "The Mother's Grief", was a eulogy to her lost son, but she never publicly explained its meaning—it was only upon Coolbrith's death that her literary friends discovered she had ever been a mother.[6] In 1862, Coolbrith moved with her mother, stepfather and twin half-brothers to San Francisco to ward off depression, and changed her name from Josephine Donna Carsley to Ina Coolbrith.[6]

2.6.2 Poet

Coolbrith soon met Bret Harte and Samuel Langhorne Clemens, writing as Mark Twain, in San Francisco.[10]

Coolbrith in San Francisco at the age of 29 or 30

In 1867, four of Coolbrith's poems appeared in *The Galaxy*.[16] In July 1868, Coolbrith supplied a poem, "Longing", for the first issue of the *Overland Monthly*, and served unofficially as co-editor with Harte in selecting poems, articles and stories for the periodical. She became a friend of actress and poet Adah Menken,[4] adding to Menken's credibility as an intellectual, but was unable to impress Harte of Menken's worth.[17] Coolbrith also worked as a schoolteacher for extra income. For a decade, Coolbrith supplied one poem for each new issue of the *Overland Monthly*.[18] After the 1866 publication of four of her poems in an anthology edited by Harte, Coolbrith's "The Mother's Grief" was positively reviewed in *The New York Times*.[19] Another poem, "When the Grass Shall Cover Me", appeared unattributed in an anthology of John Greenleaf Whittier's favorite works by other poets, entitled *Songs of Three Centuries* (1875); Coolbrith's poem was judged the best of that group.[20] In 1867, recently widowed Josephine Clifford arrived at the *Overland Monthly* to take a position as secretary. She formed a lifetime friendship with Coolbrith.[21]

Coolbrith's literary work connected her with poet Alfred Lord Tennyson and naturalist John Muir, as well as Charles Warren Stoddard who also helped Harte edit the *Overland Monthly*. As editors and arbiters of literary taste, Harte, Stoddard and Coolbrith were known as the "Golden

Gate Trinity".[22] Stoddard once said that Coolbrith never had any of her literary submissions returned from a publisher.[20] Coolbrith met writer and critic Ambrose Bierce in 1869, and by 1871 when he was courting Mary Ellen Day, Bierce organized friendly card games between himself, Day, Coolbrith and Stoddard. Bierce felt that Coolbrith's best poems were "California", the commencement ode she wrote for the University of California in 1871, and "Beside the Dead", written in 1875.[11]

Joaquin Miller in the 1870s

In mid-1870, Coolbrith met the eccentric poet Cincinnatus Hiner Miller, newly divorced from his second wife, and introduced him to the San Francisco literary circle at the suggestion of Stoddard. Miller quoted Tennyson in describing Coolbrith as "divinely tall, and most divinely fair".[15][23] Coolbrith discovered that Miller was appreciative of the heroic, tragic life of Joaquin Murrieta, and she suggested that Miller take the name Joaquin Miller as his pen name, and that he dress the part with longer hair and a more-pronounced mountain man costume.[10] Coolbrith helped Miller prepare for his trip to England, where he would lay a laurel wreath on the tomb of Lord Byron, a poet they both greatly admired.[20] The two gathered California Bay Laurel branches in Sausalito and took portrait photographs together. Coolbrith wrote "With a Wreath of Laurel" about this enterprise.[15] Miller went to New York by train, calling himself "Joaquin Miller" for the first time,[24] and was in London by August 1870. When he placed the wreath

at the Church of St. Mary Magdalene, Hucknall, it caused a stir among the English clergy who did not see any connection between California poets and the late lord. They sent to Constantine I, the King of Greece for another laurel wreath from that country of Byron's heroic death, accompanied by some Greek funding which was joined in kind from the purse of the Bishop of Norwich to rebuild and refurbish the 500-year-old church. The two wreaths were hung side by side over Byron's tomb.[20]

2.6.3 Librarian

Coolbrith had hoped to tour the East Coast and Europe with Miller, but stayed behind in San Francisco because she felt obliged to care for her mother and her seriously ill, widowed sister Agnes who was unable to care for herself or for her two children. In late 1871 she took on the care of another dependent when Joaquin Miller brought her a teenaged Indian girl (widely rumored to be his own daughter) to care for while he went abroad again, this time to Brazil and Europe.[24]

Beside the Dead

It must be sweet, O thou, my dead, to lie
With hands that folded are from every task;
Sealed with the seal of the great mystery,
The lips that nothing answer, nothing ask.
The life-long struggle ended; ended quite
The weariness of patience, and of pain,
And the eyes closed to open not again
On desolate dawn or dreariness of night.
It must be sweet to slumber and forget;
To have the poor tired heart so still at last;
Done with all yearning, done with all regret,
Doubt, fear, hope, sorrow, all forever past;
Past all the hours, or slow of wing or fleet—
It must be sweet, it must be very sweet!

—Ina Coolbrith[1]

At a literary dinner on May 5, 1874, Coolbrith was elected honorary member of the Bohemian Club,[25] the second of four women so honored.[26] This allowed the members of the club to discreetly assist her in her finances, but their help was not enough to cover her full burden. Coolbrith moved to Oakland to set up a larger household for her extended family. Coolbrith's sister Agnes died late in 1874, and the orphaned niece and nephew continued to live with Coolbrith.[15] Coolbrith wrote "Beside the Dead" in grief from the loss of her sister. Her mother Agnes died in 1876.[3]

To support the household, in late 1874 Coolbrith took a position as the librarian for the Oakland Library Association, a subscription library that had been established five years earlier. In 1878, the library was reformed as the Oakland Free Library, the second public library created in California under the Rogers Free Library Act (Eureka was first).[27] Coolbrith earned a salary of $80 per month, $1,960 in current value, much less than a man would have received. She worked 6 days a week, 12 hours a day. Her poetry suffered as a result. She published only sporadically over the next 19 years[15]—working as Oakland's librarian was the low point of her poetic career.[12]

"...I named you 'Noble'. That is what you were to me—noble. That was the feeling I got from you. Oh, yes, I got, also, the feeling of sorrow and suffering, but dominating them, always riding above all, was noble. No woman has so affected me to the extent you did. I was only a little lad. I knew absolutely nothing about you. Yet in all the years that have passed I have met no woman so noble as you."
—Jack London, in a letter to Coolbrith[28]

At the library, her style was personal: she discussed with the patrons their interests, and she selected books she felt were appropriate. In 1886, she befriended and mentored the 10-year-old Jack London, guiding his reading. London called her his "literary mother". Twenty years later, London wrote to Coolbrith to thank her.[28]

Coolbrith also mentored young Isadora Duncan[29] who later described Coolbrith as "a very wonderful" woman, with "very beautiful eyes that glowed with burning fire and passion".[28] Magazine writer Samuel Dickson reported that, at a soirée in 1927, an aging Coolbrith told him of the famous lovers she had known, and that she had once dazzled Joseph Duncan, Isadora's father. Coolbrith said that his attentions led to the breakup of his marriage. Duncan's mother left San Francisco and settled her four children in Oakland, little knowing that Coolbrith would soon meet one of her children, and help the young dancer develop a wider knowledge of the world through reading.[30] Duncan wrote in her autobiography that, as a librarian, Coolbrith was always pleased with the youthful dancer's book choices, and that Duncan did not find out until later that Coolbrith was "evidently the great passion of [Joseph Duncan's] life".[31]

Coolbrith's nephew Henry Frank Peterson came to work with her at the library, and began to organize the books into a faceted classification scheme that she specified, one which used one- and two-digit numbers to stand for general subjects, and three-digit numbers to indicate individual books in that subject.[32] Before this, Coolbrith had resisted library trustee attempts to classify the books; she had wished to continue the reading-room atmosphere that she had established.[12]

In 1881, Coolbrith's poetry was published in book form, entitled *A Perfect Day, and Other Poems*. Henry Wadsworth

Longfellow, after Coolbrith's publisher sent him a copy, said "I know that California has at least one poet."[20] Of the poems, he said "I have been reading them with delight."[20] Yale poet Edward Rowland Sill, professor at the University of California and a keen critic of American literature, gave Coolbrith a letter of introduction that he wished her to send to publisher Henry Holt. It said, simply, "Miss Ina Coolbrith, one of our few really literary persons in California, and the writer of many lovely poems; in fact, the most genuine singer the West has yet produced."[33] Quaker poet and former abolitionist John Greenleaf Whittier wrote to Coolbrith from Amesbury, Massachusetts, to share his opinion that her "little volume" of poetry, "which has found such favor with all who have seen it on this side of the Rocky mountains", should be republished on the East Coast.[33] He told her "there is no verse on the Pacific Slope which has the fine quality of thine."[33]

Beginning as early as 1865 in San Francisco, Coolbrith held literary meetings at her home, hosting readings of poetry, and topical discussions, in the tradition of European salons.[22] She helped writers such as Gelett Burgess and Laura Redden Searing gain wider notice.[34]

Until he criticized her in writing, Coolbrith considered Ambrose Bierce a good friend.

Once warmly social with her, in the 1880s Ambrose Bierce turned his caustic pen to criticism of Coolbrith's work, and thus lost her as a friend.[11] In 1883, he wrote that her finely-wrought poem "Our Poets" should have been made a dirge, as the great poets of California were dead. He wrote that the periodical she worked for should be named the *Warmed-Overland Monthly* because it delivered nothing new. Regarding her poem "Unattained", Bierce complained of "this dainty writer's tiresome lugubriousness."[11]

In response, Coolbrith sided with those who said his incessant needling led local writer David Lesser Lezinsky to suicide.[11]

The Poet

He walks with God upon the hills!
And sees, each morn, the world arise
New-bathed in light of paradise.
He hears the laughter of her rills,
Her melodies of many voices,
And greets her while his heart rejoices.
She to his spirit undefiled,
Makes answer as a little child;
Unveiled before his eyes she stands,
And gives her secret to his hands.

—Ina Coolbrith[1]

Coolbrith published poems in *The Century* in 1883, 1885, 1886 and 1894.[35] All four poems were included in Coolbrith's 1895 book, *Songs from the Golden Gate*—a reissue of her earlier 1881 collection, with some 40 poems added.[1] In New York, Coolbrith was acknowledged by a reviewer in the monthly journal *Current Opinion* as "a true, melodious and natural singer. Her work is characterized by great delicacy and refinement of feeling, and comprises dainty love songs, verses of deep religious feeling, stately odes, written for special occasions, and charming bits of description."[1]

In September 1892, Coolbrith was given three days' notice to clear her desk, to be replaced as librarian by her nephew Henry Frank Peterson.[12] A library trustee was quoted as saying "we need a librarian not a poet."[12] Coolbrith's literary friends were outraged, and published a lengthy opinion piece to that effect in the *San Francisco Examiner*.[20] Peterson's plans for the library were quite successful, however; under his guidance circulation quickly grew from 3,000 to 13,000.[12] Peterson opened the library on Sundays and holidays and increased accessibility to the stacks—he was praised by trustees for his "management improvements".[12]

In 1893 at the World's Congress of Representative Women, held at the beginning of the World's Columbian Exposition in Chicago, Coolbrith was described by Ella Sterling Cummins (later Mighels) as "the best known of California writers... who stands peerless at the head."[36] Coolbrith was commissioned to write a poem for the Exposition, and in October 1893 she brought with her to Chicago the poem "Isabella of Spain" to help dedicate Harriet Hosmer's sculpture *Queen Isabella* which stood before the Pampas Plume Palace within the California Pavilion.[37] Listening to Coolbrith were well-known women such as suffragist Susan B. Anthony and journalist Lilian Whiting.[38] During Coolbrith's visit, Charlotte Perkins Stetson, her friend from the Pacific Coast Woman's Press Association (the two women served as president and vice-president, respectively), wrote to May Wright Sewall on her behalf; Stetson observed that Coolbrith could benefit from introductions to Chicago's best writers.[39]

Coolbrith's difficulties in Oakland followed by her trip to Chicago unsettled her friends who did not wish to see her move away and "become an alien" to California.[40] John Muir had long been in the habit of sending Coolbrith letters, and the occasional box of fruit such as cherries picked from the trees on his Martinez estate, and he made such an offering in late 1894, accompanied by a suggestion for a new career which he thought would keep her in the area—she could fill the position of San Francisco's librarian, recently vacated by John Vance Cheney. Coolbrith sent a response to Muir, thanking him for "the fruit of your land, and the fruit of your brain".[41] After signing the letter "your old-time friend", she added a post-script comment: "No, I cannot have Mr. Cheney's place. I am *disqualified by sex*."[41] San Francisco required that their librarian be a man.

In 1894, Coolbrith honored poet Celia Thaxter with a memorial poem entitled "The Singer of the Sea". Thaxter had been to the *Atlantic Monthly* what Coolbrith was to the *Overland Monthly*: its "lady poet" who submitted verse containing "local color".[42]

The Sea-Shell

"And love will stay, a summer's day!"
A long wave rippled up the strand,
She flashed a white hand through the spray
And plucked a sea-shell from the sand;
And laughed—"O doubting heart, have peace!
When faith of mine shall fail to thee
This fond, remembering shell will cease
To sing its love, the sea."
Ah, well! sweet summer's past and gone,—
And love, perchance, shuns wintry weather,—
And so the pretty dears are flown
On lightsome, careless wings together.
I smile: this little pearly-lined,
Pink-veined shell she gave to me,
With foolish, faithful lips to find
Still sing its love, the sea.

—Ina Coolbrith[43]

A second poetry collection, *Songs from the Golden Gate*, was published in 1895; it contained "The Mariposa Lily", a description of California's natural beauty, and "The Captive of the White City" which detailed the cruelty dealt to Native Americans in the late 19th century.[4] As well, the collection included "The Sea-Shell" and "Sailed", two poems in which Coolbrith described a woman's love with deep sympathy and an unusually vivid physical imagery, in a way that presaged the later Imagist school of Ezra Pound and Robert Frost.[4] The book included four monochrome reproductions of paintings by William Keith that he had devised as visual representations of the poetry. The book was well received in London where editor Albert Kinross of *The Outlook* papered the London Underground walls with posters announcing "his great discovery".[44]

Connections among Coolbrith's circle of friends resulted in a librarian job at San Francisco's Mercantile Library Association in 1898, and she moved back to Russian Hill in San Francisco. In January 1899, artist William Keith and poet Charles Keeler obtained for her a part-time position as librarian of the Bohemian Club, of which Keith and Keeler were members. Her first assignment was to edit *Songs from Bohemia*, a book of poems by Daniel O'Connell, Bohemian Club co-founder and journalist, following his death.[45] Her salary was $50 each month,[25] less than she had been earning in Oakland, but her duties were light enough that she was able to devote a greater proportion of her time to writing, and she signed on as sometime staff of Charles Fletcher Lummis's *The Land of Sunshine* magazine.[46] As a personal project, she began to work on a history of California literature.

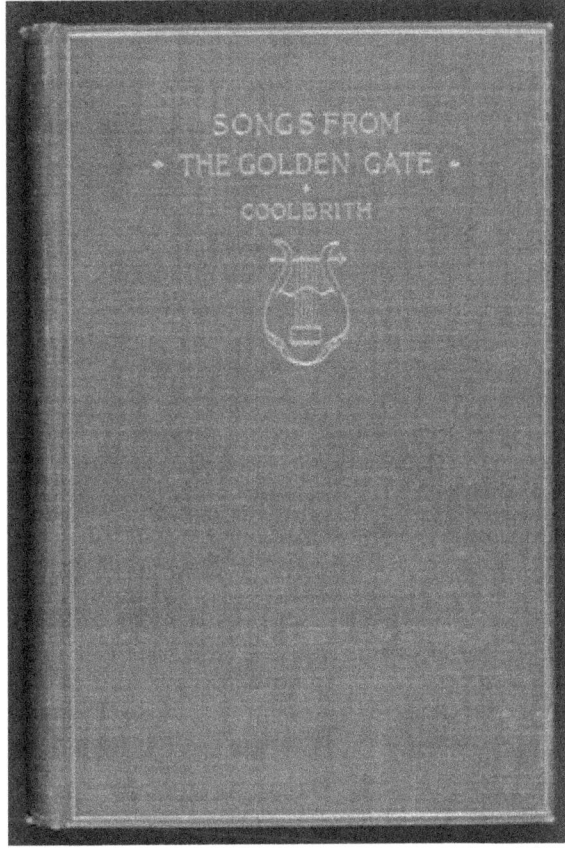

Songs from the Golden Gate *(1895)*

2.6.4 Earthquake and fire

By February 1906, Coolbrith's health was showing signs of deterioration. She was often sick in bed with rheumatism, and hard-pressed to continue her work at the Bohemian Club.[18] Still, in March 1906 she gave a lengthy reading to the Pacific Coast Woman's Press Association entitled "Some Women Poets of America." Coolbrith, third vice president and life member of the club, briefly discussed the most prominent early American women poets but focused more fully on ones that became known in the second half of the 19th century, reciting example verse, and critically evaluating the work.[47] A month later, disaster struck in the form of calamitous fire following the April 1906 San Francisco earthquake: Coolbrith's home at 1604 Taylor Street burned to the ground. Directly after the earthquake but before fire threatened, Coolbrith left her house carrying a pet cat, thinking she would soon return. Her student boarder Robert Norman and her companion Josephine Zeller[48] were unable to carry more than another cat, a few small bundles of letters and Coolbrith's scrapbook. Immediately after he spotted heavy smoke from across the bay, Joaquin Miller took the ferry from Oakland to San Francisco in order to assist Coolbrith in saving her valuables from encroaching fire, but was prevented from doing so by soldiers who had orders to use deadly force against looters.[18] In the blaze,

Coolbrith lost 3,000 books including priceless signed first editions, artwork by Keith, many personal letters from famous people such as Whittier, Clemens, George Meredith and, above all, her nearly complete manuscript that was part autobiography and part history of California's early literary scene.

"Were I to write what I know, the book would be too sensational to print, but were I to write what I think proper, it would be too dull to read."
—Ina Coolbrith, on the absence of an autobiography[49]

Coolbrith never resumed the work of writing the history,[10] as she was unable to balance its revelatory autobiographical truth with the scandal that would then ensue. In her life, there were rumors that she had accepted men such as Harte, Stoddard, Clemens and Miller as occasional lovers— a book discussing these liaisons was one she considered too controversial.[49]

Coolbrith spent a few years in temporary residences while friends rallied to raise money to build a house for her. From New York, Coolbrith's old associate Mark Twain sent three autographed photographs of himself that sold for $10 apiece—he was subsequently convinced to sit for 17 more studio photographs to add further to the fund.[50] In

February 1907, the San Jose Women's Club hosted an event called "Ina Coolbrith Day" to promote interest in legislating a state pension for Coolbrith, and in a book project being put forward by the Spinners' Club. In June 1907, the Spinners' Club printed a book entitled *The Spinners' book of fiction*[51] whose proceeds were to be given to Coolbrith. Frank Norris, Mary Hallock Foote and Mary Hunter Austin were among the authors who contributed stories. The poet George Sterling, a friend from the Bohemian Club, submitted an introductory poem, and Bohemian Maynard Dixon was among the illustrators. The driving force behind the effort was Gertrude Atherton, a writer who saw in Coolbrith a connection to California's literary origins. When the book failed to produce sufficient funding, Atherton added enough from her own pocket to start construction. A new house was built for Coolbrith at 1067 Broadway on Russian Hill.[28][52] Settled, there, she resumed hosting salons. In 1910, she received a trust fund from Atherton.[53] During 1910–1914, with money from Atherton and a discreet grant from her Bohemian friends,[54] Coolbrith spent time going between residences in New York City and in San Francisco, writing poetry.[18] In four winters, she wrote more poetry than in the preceding 25 years.[54]

2.6.5 Poet laureate

In 1911, Coolbrith accepted the presidency of the Pacific Coast Woman's Press Association, and a park was dedicated to her, at 1715 Taylor Street, one block from her pre-earthquake home. Coolbrith was named honorary member of the California Writers Club around 1913, a group that quickly expanded to include Lummis and other Southern Californians.[55] In 1913, Ella Sterling Mighels founded the California Literature Society which met informally once a month at Coolbrith's Russian Hill home, newspaper columnist and literary critic George Hamlin Fitch presiding. Mighels, who has been called California's literary historian, credited her breadth of knowledge to Coolbrith and the society meetings.[44]

In preparation for the 1915 Panama–Pacific International Exposition in San Francisco, Coolbrith was named President of the Congress of Authors and Journalists. In this position she sent more than 4,000 letters to the world's most well-known writers and journalists. At the Exposition itself on June 30, Coolbrith was lauded by Senator James D. Phelan who said that her early associate Bret Harte called her the "sweetest note in California literature."[14] Phelan continued, "she has written little, but that little is great. It is of the purest quality, finished and perfect, as well as full of feeling and thought."[14] The *Overland Monthly* reported that "eyes were wet throughout the large audience"[14] when Coolbrith was crowned with a laurel wreath by Benjamin Ide Wheeler, President of the University of California, who

Portrait of Coolbrith from a publication of her poem California, *1918*

called her the "loved, laurel-crowned poet of California."[28] After several more speeches were made in her honor, and bouquets brought in abundance to the podium, Coolbrith, wearing a black robe with a sash bearing a garland of bright orange California poppies, addressed the crowd, saying, "There is one woman here with whom I want to share these honors: Josephine Clifford McCracken. For we are linked together, the last two living members of Bret Harte's staff of *Overland* writers."[56] McCracken was then ushered up from her seat in the audience to join Coolbrith.[14] Coolbrith's official status as California Poet Laureate was confirmed in 1919 as the "Loved Laurel Crowned Poet of California"[57] by the California State Senate with no financial support attached.[12]

Several months after the San Francisco fair, at the Panama–California Exposition held in San Diego, festivities included a series of Authors' Days, featuring 13 California writers. November 2, 1915, was "Ina Coolbrith Day": her poems were recited, a lecture on her life was given by George Wharton James, and her poetry was set to music and performed on piano and voice, with compositions by James, Humphrey John Stewart, and Amy Beach.[58]

Coolbrith continued to write and work to support herself. From 1909 to final publication in 1917, she painstakingly collected and edited a book of Stoddard's poetry, writing a foreword and joining her short memorial poem "At Anchor" to verse submitted by Stoddard's friends Joaquin Miller, George Sterling and Thomas Walsh.[59] At the age of 80, McCracken wrote to Coolbrith to complain to her dear friend of still having to work for a living: "The world has not used us well, Ina; California has been ungrateful to us. Of all the hundred thousands the state pays out in pensions of one kind and another, don't you think you should be at the head of the pensioners, and I somewhere down below?"[60]

2.6.6   Death and legacy

Coolbrith portrait by Ansel Adams

In May 1923, Coolbrith's friend Edwin Markham found her at the Hotel Latham in New York, "very old, ill and moneyless".[61] He asked Lotta Crabtree to gather help for her. Crippled with arthritis, Coolbrith was brought back to California where she settled in Berkeley to be cared for by her niece. In 1924, Mills College conferred upon her an honorary Master of Arts degree.[28] Coolbrith published

Retrospect: In Los Angeles in 1925.[62] In April 1926, she received visitors such as her old friend, art patron Albert M. Bender, who brought young Ansel Adams to meet her.[49] Adams made a photographic portrait of Coolbrith seated near one of her white Persian cats and wearing a large white mantilla on her head.[7]

Coolbrith died on Leap Day, February 29, 1928, and was buried in Mountain View Cemetery in Oakland. Her grave (located in Plot 11 at 37°50′00″N 122°14′20″W / 37.8332°N 122.2390°W) was unmarked until 1986 when a literary society known as The Ina Coolbrith Circle placed a headstone.[10] Her name is commemorated by Mount Ina Coolbrith,[63] a 7,900-foot (2,400 m) peak near Beckwourth Pass in the Sierra Nevada mountains near State Route 70. Near her Russian Hill home, Ina Coolbrith Park, established earlier as a series of terraces ascending a steep hill, received a memorial plaque placed in 1947 by the San Francisco parlors of the Native Daughters of the Golden West. The park is known for its "meditative setting and spectacular bay views".[64]

Wings of Sunset, a book of Coolbrith's later poetry, was published in the year after her death. Charles Joseph MacConaghy Phillips edited the collection, and wrote a brief memorial to Coolbrith's life.[65]

In 1933, the University of California established the Ina Coolbrith Memorial Poetry Prize, given annually to authors of the best unpublished poems written by undergraduate students enrolled at the University of the Pacific, Mills College, Stanford University, Santa Clara University, Saint Mary's College of California, and any of the University of California campuses.[66]

In 1965, the actress June Lockhart played Coolbrith in the episode "Magic Locket" of the syndicated western television series, *Death Valley Days*, hosted by Ronald W. Reagan. In the story line, Coolbrith develops a tenuous friendship with the teen-aged "Dorita Duncan" (Kathy Garver), later the dancer Isadora Duncan. The two have identical portions of a broken locket. Sean McClory played the poet Joaquin Miller, author of *Songs of the Sierras*.[67]

The California Writers Club (CWC) occasionally selects a member, one distinguished by "exemplary service", to receive the Ina Coolbrith Award. In 2009, the award was given to Joyce Krieg, editor of the *CWC Bulletin*. In 2011, Kelly Harrison received the award for work on the anthology *West Winds Centennial*.[68][69] In his 1997 novel *Separations*, author Oakley Hall set Coolbrith and others of her 1870 literary circle as main characters in the story.[22] Hall was sympathetic to Coolbrith's legacy, himself helping to develop new California writers through the forum Squaw Valley Writer's Conference.[70]

In 2001, a $63,000 sculpture by Scott Donahue was

The Ina Coolbrith Circle emplaced this laurel wreath-engraved headstone in 1986.

placed in Oakland's central Frank Ogawa Plaza, adjacent to Oakland City Hall. The artist said his 13-foot-2-inch (4.01 m) polychrome patchwork statue was a composite image of 20 women, historic and current, important to Oakland, including Coolbrith, Isadora Duncan, Julia Morgan and more.[71] Entitled *Sigame/Follow Me*, the sculpture elicited protests because the city did not follow its own process for acquiring public art and because "some people", according to Ben Hazard, Oakland's Craft and Cultural Arts Department leader, "just don't like the sculpture's looks".[72] By late 2004, the sculpture had been removed to a remote former industrial site called Union Point Park on the Oakland Estuary, opening to the public in 2005.[73]

The City of Berkeley in 2003 installed a series of 120 poem-imprinted cast-iron plates flanking one block of a downtown street, to become the Addison Street Poetry Walk.[74] Former U.S. Poet Laureate Robert Hass determined that one of Coolbrith's works should be included. A 55-pound (25 kg) plate bearing Coolbrith's poem "Copa De Oro (The California Poppy)"[75] in raised porcelain enamel text is set into the sidewalk at the high-traffic northwest corner of Addison and Shattuck Avenues.[76]

2.6.7   See also

- List of descendants of Joseph Smith, Sr. and Lucy Mack Smith

2.6.8   References

Notes

[1] "American Poets of To-Day: Ina Coolbrith". *Current Opinion* (The Current Literature Publishing Co.) **28** (1): 16–17. April 1900.

[2] Western Literature Association (1987). J. Golden Taylor, ed. *A Literary history of the American West*. TCU Press. p. 181. ISBN 0-87565-021-X.

[3] Moulton, Charles Wells (1889). "Ina D. Coolbrith". *The Magazine of Poetry and Literary Review* (Buffalo, New York) **1**: 312–315.

[4] Axelrod, 2003, p. 610

[5] Muske-Dukes, Carol (December 12, 2008). "Single laurel, common voice". *Los Angeles Times*. Retrieved March 20, 2010.

[6] Egli, 1997, p. 215.

[7] Herny, 2008, p. 20.

[8] Historian Todd Compton counts Fanny Alger as a wife of Joseph Smith, but George D. Smith and Fawn M. Brodie do not.

- Brodie, Fawn (1971). *No Man Knows My History*. New York: Alfred A. Knopf. ISBN 0-679-73054-0.

- Compton, Todd (Summer 1996). "A Trajectory of Plurality: An Overview of Joseph Smith's Thirty-three Plural Wives". *Dialogue: A Journal of Mormon Thought* **29** (2): 1–38.

- Smith, George D. (Spring 1994). "Nauvoo Roots of Mormon Polygamy, 1841–46: A Preliminary Demographic Report". *Dialogue: A Journal of Mormon Thought* **27** (1).

[9] Compton, Todd (1997). *In Sacred Loneliness: the plural wives of Joseph Smith*. Signature Books. p. 170. ISBN 1-56085-085-X.

[10] Albert, Janice. "Ina Coolbrith (1841–1928) and the California Frontier". *California Authors*. California Association of Teachers of English. Retrieved February 20, 2010.

[11] Gale, Robert L. (2001). *An Ambrose Bierce companion*. Greenwood Publishing Group. pp. 57–58. ISBN 0-313-31130-7.

[12] Redman, Joe (2006). "The Dismissal of Ina Coolbrith Revisited". Retrieved February 20, 2010.

[13] "Guide to the Ina Donna Coolbrith Collection". *The Bancroft Library*. Online Archive of California. Retrieved February 19, 2010.

[14] Taylor, Marian (November 1915). "Congress of Authors and Journalists at the Panama-Pacific International Exposition". *Overland Monthly* (San Francisco) **LXVI** (5): 439–447.

[15] Herny, 2008, pp. 22–23.

[16] Library of Congress, American Memory. Cornell University.
Coolbrith, Ina (February 1867). "Who Knoweth?". *The Galaxy* **3** (4).
Coolbrith, Ina (April 1867). "At Peace". *The Galaxy* **3** (7).
Coolbrith, Ina (June 1867). "Among The Daisies". *The Galaxy* **4** (2).
Coolbrith, Ina (July 1867). "Wearisome". *The Galaxy* **4** (3).

[17] Sentilles, Renée M. (2003). *Performing Menken: Adah Isaacs Menken and the birth of American celebrity*. Cambridge University Press. pp. 177, 189. ISBN 0-521-82070-7.

[18] George, Aleta. "Ina Coolbrith's Lost City of Love and Desire". Oakland, California: The Ina Coolbrith Circle. Retrieved February 20, 2010.

[19] Egli, 1997, p. xix.

[20] "A Poet's Literary Friends, Their Answers to the Question, 'What Has Ina Coolbrith Done?'". *San Francisco Examiner*. November 27, 1892. Newspaper clipping found inside *A Perfect Day, and Other Poems*, by Ina D. Coolbrith. 1881.

[21] Egli, 1997, p. 111.

[22] Hicks, Jack (2000). *The Literature of California: Native American beginnings to 1945*. University of California Press. p. 228. ISBN 0-520-21524-9.

[23] Tennyson, Alfred (1903). Henry Van Dyke, ed. *Poems of Tennyson*. The Athenaeum Press Series. Boston: Ginn. p. 56.

[24] Guilford-Kardell, Margaret; McKeown, Scott (August 2008). "Readers' Updates of the Joaquin Miller Timeline" (PDF). *Margaret Guilford-Kardell's Bibliography on the Life, Times, and Exploits of Cincinnatus Hiner Miller*. JoaquinMiller.com. Retrieved March 2, 2010.

[25] Wood, Raymund F. (1958). "Ina Coolbrith, librarian". *California Librarian* (California Library Association) **19**: 102–104.

[26] "Honorary Members". *Constitution and by-laws of the Bohemian club of San Francisco*. Bohemian Club. 1895. p. 58. Coolbrith was second of the four women given honorary membership in the club. The first honorary female member was Margaret B. Bowman, wife of club co-founder James F. Bowman, she being elected by acclamation during the first formal Bohemian Club meeting. By 1895, three more women were honorary members, including Coolbrith in 1874, author Sara Jane Lippincott (pseudonym Grace Greenwood), and actress Elizabeth Crocker Bowers, wife of actor David P. Bowers. Coolbrith outlived them to become the last female club member.

[27] "History". Oakland Public Library. Retrieved July 8, 2009.

[28] Hartzell, David. "Jack London's Literary Mother". JackLondons.net. Retrieved February 20, 2010.

[29] Daly, Ann (1995). *Done Into Dance*. Indiana University Press. p. 12. ISBN 0-253-32924-8.

[30] Dickson, Samuel (1949). "Isadora Duncan (1878–1927)". The Virtual Museum of the City of San Francisco. Retrieved July 9, 2009.

[31] Duncan, Isadora (1927). *My Life* (4 ed.). Boni and Liveright. p. 22.

[32] Miel, Charles L., trustee (April 1885). *Catalogue of the Oakland Free Public Library*. Ina Coolbrith, librarian; Henry F. Peterson, first assistant librarian. Oakland, California: Tribune Publishing Company. Retrieved February 22, 2010.

[33] Loughead, Flora Haines (July 1902). "Books and Writers". *Sunset Magazine* **IX**: 217–219.

[34] Glyndon, Howard (2003). *Sweet bells jangled*. Gallaudet University Press. p. 14. ISBN 1-56368-138-2.

[35] Library of Congress, American Memory. Cornell University.
Coolbrith, Ina (March 1883). "February". *The Century* **25** (5).
Coolbrith, Ina (December 1885). "The Poet". *The Century* **31** (2).
Coolbrith, Ina (February 1886). "Retrospect". *The Century* **31** (4).
Coolbrith, Ina (October 1894). "The Flight of Song". *The Century* **48** (6).

[36] Cummins, Ella Sterling (1893). "The Women Writers of California". *The Congress of Women*. Retrieved February 20, 2010.

[37] Silver, Mae (March 17, 1994). "1894 Midwinter Fair: Women Artists". Clover Leaf Media. Archived from the original on May 27, 2008. Retrieved January 26, 2010. Check date values in: |year= / |date= mismatch (help)

[38] Cook, Joel (1891–1893). "Reception in Honor of Harriet Hosmer's Statue of Isabella". *The World's Fair at Chicago*. Rand, McNally & Co.

[39] Stetson, Charlotte Perkins. "Letter from Charlotte Perkins Stetson to May Wright Sewall". *The May Wright Sewall Papers*. Retrieved July 9, 2009.

[40] Stedman, Edmund Clarence (December 1893). "Books and Authors". *The Californian Illustrated Magazine* (Charles Frederick Holder) **V** (1): 284.

[41] Coolbrith, Ina. "Letter from Ina Coolbrith to John Muir, November 19, 1894.". *Collection of letters to John Muir*. Online Archive of California. Retrieved February 22, 2010.

[42] Patterson, Daniel; Thompson, Roger; Bryson, J. Scott (2008). *Early American nature writers*. Greenwood Publishing Group. p. 328. ISBN 0-313-34680-1.

[43] Coolbrith, Ina (1895). *Songs from the Golden Gate*. Boston and New York: Houghton, Mifflin and Company. p. 52.

[44] Mighels, Ella Sterling (1918). *Literary California: Poetry, Prose and Portraits*. San Francisco: Harr Wagner Publishing. pp. 19, 27.

[45] O'Connell, Daniel (1900). *Songs from Bohemia*. A. M. Robertson.

[46] Lummis, Charles F. (December 1899 to May 1900). *The Land of Sunshine* (Los Angeles, California: Land of Sunshine Publishing) **XII** https://archive.org/stream/outwestland12archrich#page/n10/mode/1up. Check date values in: |date= (help); Missing or empty |title= (help); |chapter= ignored (help)

[47] "P.C.W.P.A". *Club Life* (The Clubwoman's Guild) **4** (7): 7. March 1906.

[48] Leider, 1991, p. 217.

[49] Spaulding, Jonathan (1998). *Ansel Adams and the American Landscape*. University of California Press. p. 59. ISBN 0-520-21663-6.

[50] James, George Wharton (May 1919). "Mark Twain—An Appreciation of His Pioneer Writings on Fasting and Health (Part I)". *Physical Culture*. Twainquotes.com. Retrieved March 21, 2010.

[51] Spinners' Club (1907). *The Spinners' Book of Fiction*. Spinners' Club.

[52] Leider, 1991, p. 218.

[53] Leider, 1991, p. 219.

[54] Herny, 2008, p. 31.

[55] "About CWC: History". California Writers Club. Retrieved July 8, 2009.

[56] McCracken, Josephine Clifford (November 1915). "Ina Coolbrith Invested With Poets' Crown". *Overland Monthly* (San Francisco) **LXVI** (5): 448–450.

[57] "California Poet Laureate". Sacramento, California: California Arts Council. 2009. Archived from the original on February 18, 2010. Retrieved February 23, 2010.

[58] James, George Wharton; Bertha Bliss Tyler (1917). *Exposition Memories*. The Radiant life press. pp. 63–64.

[59] Stoddard, Charles Warren (1917). Ina Coolbrith, ed. *Poems of Charles Warren Stoddard*. John Lane company.

[60] Egli, 1997, p. 113.

[61] Guilford-Kardell, Margaret; McKeown, Scott (2006). "A Joaquin Miller Chronological Bibliography and Study Guide" (PDF). *Margaret Guilford-Kardell's Bibliography on the Life, Times, and Exploits of Cincinnatus Hiner Miller*. JoaquinMiller.com. Retrieved March 2, 2010.

[62] Coolbrith, Ina Donna; Dawson, Ernest; Nash, John Henry (1925). *Retrospect: In Los Angeles*. John Henry Nash.

[63] Brown, Thomas P. (May 30, 1940). "Over the Sierra". *Indian Valley Record*. p. 3. Retrieved 7 May 2015.

[64] Fodor's (2006). *Fodor's 2007 San Francisco*. Fodor's Gold Guides (2 ed.). Random House. p. 62. ISBN 1-4000-1693-2.

[65] Coolbrith, Ina Donna (1929). *Wings of Sunset*. Houghton Mifflin company.

[66] "Ina Coolbrith Memorial Poetry Prize". *Financial Aid*. University of California, Berkeley. Retrieved July 8, 2009.

[67] "Magic Locket on *Death Valley Days*". Internet Movie Data Base. March 17, 1965. Retrieved August 22, 2015.

[68] "Recognition: Ina Coolbrith Award". California Writers Club. Retrieved July 8, 2009.

[69] CWCMarin (November 8, 2009). "CWC09-372 by CWC-Marin". Retrieved March 1, 2010.

[70] Benson, Heidi (May 14, 2008). "Writer Oakley Hall dies at age 87". *San Francisco Chronicle*. Retrieved July 14, 2010.

[71] Costantinou, Marianne (August 3, 2001). "Strong women of Oakland: Statute [sic] honors 20 artists, leaders". *San Francisco Chronicle*. Retrieved March 2, 2010.

[72] Hung, Melissa (December 26, 2001). "Broken Promises (page 1)". *East Bay Express*. Retrieved March 2, 2010. "Broken Promises" (page 2).

[73] Kibel, Paul Stanton (Winter 2004–2005). "Creating Open Space: Two Cases of Conflict Resolved" (PDF). *California Coast & Ocean*. Coastal Conservancy Association. p. 21. Retrieved March 2, 2010.

[74] "The Addison Street Poetry Walk". *Office of Economic Development*. City of Berkeley. Retrieved March 2, 2010.

[75] Hubbell, Dan (September 11, 2007). "Copa de oro". *Schleusenmeister's photostream on Flickr*. Yahoo!. Retrieved March 2, 2010.

[76] Hass, Robert; Fisher, Jessica (2004). *The Addison Street anthology: Berkeley's poetry walk*. Heyday Books. pp. 24–25. ISBN 1-890771-94-5.

Bibliography

- Axelrod, Steven Gould; Camille Roman; Thomas J. Travisano (2003). *The New Anthology of American Poetry: Traditions and revolutions, beginnings to 1900*, Rutgers University Press, pp. 610–616, Chapter "Ina Coolbrith". ISBN 0-8135-3162-4

- Conmy, Peter Thomas; Oakland Free Library (1969). *The Dismissal of Ina Coolbrith as Head Librarian of Oakland Free Public Library and a Discussion of the Tenure Status of Head Librarians*, Oakland Public Library

- Dickson, Samuel (1992). *Tales of San Francisco*, Stanford University Press. ISBN 0-8047-2097-5

- Egli, Ida Rae (1997). *No Rooms of Their Own: Women Writers of Early California, 1849–1869*, Berkeley, California: Heyday Books, 2nd edition. ISBN 1-890771-01-5

- Herny, Ed; Shelley Rideout; Katie Wadell (2008). *Berkeley Bohemia: Artists and Visionaries of the Early 20th Century*, Layton, Utah: Gibbs Smith. ISBN 1-4236-0085-1

- Kennedy, Kate M. (1907). "Ina Coolbrith Day", *Overland Monthly*, San Francisco: Samuel Carson.

- Leider, Emily Wortis (1991). *California's daughter: Gertrude Atherton and her times*, Stanford University Press. ISBN 0-8047-1820-2

- Rhodamel, Josephine DeWitt; Raymund Francis Wood (1973). *Ina Coolbrith, librarian and laureate of California*, Brigham Young University Press. ISBN 0-8425-1445-7

2.6.9 External links

Selected poems

- "The Mother's Grief.", 1866

- "When the Grass Shall Cover Me"

- *California*, 1871, 1918

- "With a Wreath of Laurel", 1881

- "Isabella of Spain", 1893

- "Copa De Oro (California Poppy)", 1907

- "San Francisco, April, 1906", 1914

2.7 James F. Bowman

James F. Bowman (January 21, 1826 – April 29, 1882) was a journalist and poet in Northern California, and a cofounder of the Bohemian Club. Bowman served on several newspapers in Placerville, Sacramento and San Francisco during a 24-year career. Through his contacts among San Francisco journalists, Bowman befriended Mark Twain, artist William Keith, critic Ambrose Bierce (who included an anecdote about Bowman in his own *The Devil's Dictionary*) and a great many others.[1]

James F. Bowman

Bowman occasionally appeared in public to read his own poetry, and was mentioned in the *Daily Morning Call* for giving a recitation at a 4 July celebration in San Francisco, 1864.[2] Bowman connected in 1871 with George Frederick Parsons in Sacramento at the *Record*, was encourage to write more poetry, and to publish. Bowman was subsequently subject to attempted plagiarism of his work by "literary purloiners".[3]

In 1864, Bowman picked up a regular assignment as co-editor with Bret Harte of *The Californian* newspaper. In 1865, the daily *Dramatic Chronicle* began publication in San Francisco as a theatre and literary review, under the direction of teenager brothers Charles and Michael de Young. Charles de Young began buying witty articles from writers such as drinking buddies Twain and Bowman, including a piece written anonymously by Bowman which savaged both the grandiose style of a poetry review in *The Californian* and the poetry itself, a book by Twain and Bowman's mutual friend Charles Warren Stoddard.[4] The targeted review was one written by Bowman himself.[4] In 1868, *The Californian* closed, but by then Bowman was editing both the *Dramatic Chronicle* and the Oakland *News*.[5] In August 1868, the name *Dramatic Chronicle* was shortened to *Chronicle*, and the newspaper given wider latitude in subject matter.[3]

The *Overland Monthly* began publication in 1868, and Bowman submitted poetry. In 1872, he helped form the Bohemian Club. He served as the club's secretary 1876–1878.[6]

Bowman died in 1882, and Ambrose Bierce wrote a moving elegy which was published in the *San Francisco Wasp* on May 5:[6]

2.7.1 Margaret Bowman

James Bowman was married to **Margaret B. Bowman** who "conducted a seminary for young ladies",[7] assisted by her husband who gave lectures in rhetoric and literature. Both husband and wife were very active in forming the men-only Bohemian Club in 1872, along with other journalists and artists such as Bierce, Daniel "Dan" O'Connell, Frederick Whymper and Benoni Irwin,[8] and Margaret Bowman was elected by acclamation to honorary member status at the first formal Bohemian meeting, held in the Bowman home.[7]

Margaret Bowman died on July 10, 1886, a year after an apoplectic stroke, and her funeral and burial was conducted under the auspices of the Bohemian Club. Four Bohemians served as pallbearers.[7]

2.7.2 See also

- List of Bohemian Club members

2.7.3 References

Notes

[1] Mark Twain Project. Letter from SLC to Charles Warren Stoddard, 23 April 1867, New York, N.Y. Retrieved on July 24, 2009.

[2] Twainquote.com. The San Francisco Daily Morning Call, July 6, 1864. Fourth of July. Retrieved on July 24, 2009.

[3] Mighels, Ella Sterling, (1893). *The Story of the Files: A Review of California Writers and Literature*, Cooperative printing co., pp. 58, 97, 427.

[4] Austen, Roger; John W. Crowley. *Genteel Pagan*, Univ of Massachusetts Press, 1995, p. 54. ISBN 0-87023-980-5

[5] Mark Twain Project. Editorial narrative following 18 March 1868 to Mary Mason Fairbanks. Retrieved on July 24, 2009.

[6] Bierce, Ambrose; Grenander, M. E. *Poems of Ambrose Bierce*, U of Nebraska Press, 1995, pp. xxxi–xxxii. ISBN 0-8032-6133-0

[7] University of California, Riverside. Center for Bibliographic Studies and Research. Daily Alta California, July 14, 1886. Retrieved on July 24, 2009. The second and third honorary female members were writer Sara Jane Lippincott (pseudonym Grace Greenwood) and Elizabeth Crocker Bowers, actress wife of actor David P. Bowers.

[8] Bohemian Club, 1922

Bibliography

- Bohemian Club. *Semi-centennial high jinks in the Grove*, July 28, 1922. Haig Patigian, Sire.

- Bohemian Club. *History, officers and committees, incorporation, constitution, by-laws and rules, former officers, members, in memoriam*, 1960

- Bohemian Club. *History, officers and committees, incorporation, constitution, by-laws and rules, former officers, members, in memoriam*, 1962

- Domhoff, G. William. *Bohemian Grove and Other Retreats: A Study in Ruling-Class Cohesiveness*, Harper & Row, 1975. ISBN 0-06-131880-9

- Garnett, Porter, *The Bohemian Jinks: A Treatise*, 1908

- Dunbar H. Ogden; Douglas McDermott; Robert Károly Sarlós (1990). *Theatre West: Image and Impact*. Rodopi. ISBN 90-5183-125-0.

- Scheffauer, Herman George; Arthur Weiss; Bohemian Club. *The Sons of Baldur*, Bohemian Club, 1908.

- Stephens, Henry Morse; Wallace Arthur Sabin, Charles Caldwell Dobie, Bohemian Club. *St. Patrick at Tara*, 1909 Grove play

- Wilson, Harry Leon; Domenico Brescia; Bohemian Club. *Life*, Bohemian Club, 1919.

2.8 John of Nepomuk

John of Nepomuk (or **John Nepomucene**) (Czech: *Jan Nepomucký*) (c. 1345 – March 20, 1393)[1] is the saint of Bohemia (Czech Republic), who was drowned in the Vltava river at the behest of Wenceslaus, King of the Romans and King of Bohemia. Later accounts state that he was the confessor of the queen of Bohemia and refused to divulge the secrets of the confessional. On the basis of this account, John of Nepomuk is considered the first martyr of the Seal of the Confessional, a patron against calumnies and, because of the manner of his death, a protector from floods and drowning.[1]

2.8.1   Basic biographical information

Jan Velflín (Welflin, Wölflin) z Pomuku came from the small market town of Pomuk (later renamed Nepomuk) in Bohemia, now in the Czech Republic, which belonged to the nearby Cistercian abbey. He was born in the decade 1340-1349, and he first studied at the University of Prague, then furthered his studies in canon law at the University of Padua from 1383 to 1387. In 1393 he was made the vicar-general of Saint Giles Cathedral by Jan of Jenštejn (1348–1400), who was the Archbishop of Prague from 1378 to 1396. In the same year, on March 20, he was tortured and thrown into the river Vltava from Charles Bridge in Prague at the behest of Wenceslaus, King of the Romans and King of Bohemia (as *Wenceslaus IV).*

Martyrdom of St. John Nepomuk *by Szymon Czechowicz, National Museum in Warsaw.*

At issue was the appointment of a new abbot for the rich and powerful Benedictine Abbey of Kladruby; its abbot was a territorial magnate whose resources would be crucial to Wenceslaus in his struggles with nobles. Wenceslaus at the same time was backing the Avignon papacy, whereas the Archbishop of Prague followed its rival, the pope at Rome. Contrary to the wishes of Wenceslaus, John confirmed the archbishop's candidate for Abbot of Kladruby, and was drowned on the emperor's orders on March 20, 1393.

This account is based on four contemporary documents. The first is the accusation of the king, presented to Pope Boniface IX on April 23, 1393, by Archbishop John of Jenštejn, who immediately went to Rome together with the new abbot of Kladruby.[2]

A few years later Abbott Ladolf of Sagan listed John of Nepomuk in the catalog of Sagan abbots, completed in 1398,[3] as well as in the treatise "De longævo schismate",

lib. VII, c. xix.[4]

A further document is the "Chronik des Deutschordens"/*Chronik des Landes Preussen*, a chronicle of the Teutonic Order compiled by John of Posilge, who died in 1405.[5]

In the above accusation, John of Jenštejn already calls John of Nepomuk a "saint martyr". The biography of the bishop (written by his chaplain) describes John of Nepomuk as "gloriosum Christi martyrem miraculisque coruscum" (in English: "a glorious martyr of Christ and sparkling with miracles").

Thus, the vicar put to death for defending the laws and the autonomy of the Catholic Church became revered as a saint directly after his death.

2.8.2   Later accounts

The prototypical statue of John of Nepomuk at Charles Bridge in Prague, at the site where the saint was thrown into Vltava. Made by Jan Brokoff upon a model by Matthias Rauchmiller in 1683, on the supposed 300th anniversary of the saint's death, which was until the mid-18th century presumed to had happened in 1383. It was the basis for a number of statues of the saint all across the Europe.

Much additional biographical information comes from Bohemian annalists who wrote 60 or more years after the events they recount. Although they may have taken ad-

St. John of Nepomuk Fountain in Kranj. It was made in 1911–13 by Franc Berneker.

St. John of Nepomuk in Buchach, Ukraine. Made by Johann Georg Pinsel, 1750 (copy)

vantage of sources not available today, their contribution is considered legendary by many historians, particularly by the Protestant ones.

- In his chronicle *Chronica regum Romanorum*, completed in 1459, Thomas Ebendorfer (d. 1464) states that King Wenceslaus had drowned the confessor of his wife, indicated as *Magister Jan*, because he had

stated that *only the one who rules properly deserves the name of king* and had refused to betray the seal of Confession. This is the first source to mention this refusal as the true motivation of the condemnation of John of Nepomuk.

- In his *Instructions for the King*, completed in 1471, Paul Zidek provides further details.[6] King Venceslaus was afraid that his wife had a lover. As she was used to confessing to *Magister Jan*, he ordered him to tell the name of the lover, but to no avail. Therefore, the king ordered John to be drowned. Note that in these chronicles neither the date of the events, nor the name of the queen is mentioned.

- In 1483 John of Krumlov, dean of St. Vitus cathedral, states that the Saint died in 1383 (one decade earlier than the recognized date, maybe due to a copying error).[7] As the first wife of Venceslaus died in 1386, this change of date also causes uncertainty about the name of the queen.[8]

The mistake of John of Krumlov crept into the *Annales Bohemorum*[9] of Wenceslaus Hajek of Liboczan (Václav Hájek z Libočan), the "Bohemian Livy". He suggested that two Jan di Nepomuks may have existed and have been killed by King Wenceslaus. The first one is the queen's confessor, who died in 1383; the other the vicar of the archbishop, who disagreed with the king on the election of the abbot of Kladruby and was drowned in 1393. As Hajek's annals enjoyed a wide success, they influenced all subsequent historians for two centuries, up to the Latin edition, critically annotated by the translator, which considerably reduced Hajek's credit as a reliable historian.

Further and less reliable details about John of Nepomuk come from the annalists of the 17th and 18th centuries. Boleslaus Balbinus, S.J., in his *Vita b. Joannis Nepomuceni martyris*[10] gives the most rich account.

Although the theory of Hajek of Liboczan has no credit today, some historians believe the vicar's refusal to betray the seal of the confessional might have been the secret reason why Wenceslaus took vengeance on John of Nepomuk as soon as a credible excuse provided the opportunity.

2.8.3 A controversial figure

Catholics see John of Nepomuk as a martyr to the cause of defending the Seal of the Confessional, romantic nationalists regard him as a Czech martyr to imperial interference, and most historians present him as a victim of a late version of the inveterate investiture controversy between secular rulers and the Catholic hierarchy.

1732 monument on Cathedral Island in Wrocław, by Jan Jiři Urbansky

The place on the bridge parapet where John of Nepomuk was thrown into the Vltava.

The connection of John of Nepomuk with the inviolability of the confessional is part of the transformation of an historical figure into a legend, which can be traced through successive stages. The archbishop, who hastened to Rome soon after the crime, in his charge against Wenceslaus, called the victim a martyr; in the *vita* written a few years later miracles are already recorded, by which the drowned man was discovered. About the middle of the 15th century the statement appears for the first time that the refusal to violate the seal of confession was the cause of John's death. Two decades later (1471), the dean of Prague, Paul Zidek, makes John the queen's confessor. The chronicler Wenceslaus Hajek speaks in 1541 (perhaps due to an incorrect reading of his sources) of *two* Johns of Nepomuk being drowned; the first as confessor, the second for his confirmation of the abbot.

The legend is especially indebted for its growth to the Jesuit historiographer Boleslaus Balbinus the "Bohemian Pliny", whose *Vita beati Joannis Nepomuceni martyris* was published in Prague, 1670. Although the Prague metropolitan chapter did not accept the biography dedicated to it, "as being frequently destitute of historical foundation and erroneous, a bungling work of mythological rhetoric", Balbinus stuck to it. In 1683 the Charles Bridge was adorned with a statue of the saint, which has had numerous successors; in 1708 the first church was dedicated to him at Hradec

Králové; a more famous Pilgrimage Church of Saint John of Nepomuk was founded in 1719.

Meanwhile, in spite of the objection of the Jesuits, the process was inaugurated which ended with his canonization. On May 31, 1721, he was beatified, and on March 19, 1729, he was canonized under Pope Benedict XIII. The acts of the process, comprising 500 pages, distinguish two Johns of Nepomuk and sanction the *cult* of the one who was drowned in 1383 as a martyr of the sacrament of penance.

According to some Protestant sources, the figure of St. John Nepomuk is a legend due to Jesuits and that its historical kernel is really Jan Hus, who was metamorphosed from a Bohemian Reformer into a Roman Catholic saint: the Nepomuk story would be based on Wenceslaus Hajek's blending of the Jan who was drowned in 1393 and the Jan who was burned in 1415. The resemblances are certainly striking, extending to the manner of celebrating their commemorations. But when the Jesuits came to Prague, the Nepomuk veneration had long been widespread; and the idea of canonization originated in opposition not to the Hussites, but to Protestantism, as a weapon of the Counter-Reformation. In the image of the saint which gradually arose is reflected the religious history of Bohemia.

A coincidental drought in the region a year later helped the legend along; the church convinced the peasants that the drought represented God's punishment for the killing of Jan Nepomucký. Building on that success, they attempted to paint the king as even blacker, with certain clerical circles spreading reports of John's courage, saying that as confessor to the Queen he had refused to reveal her secrets, and that was why he had been murdered. Belief in John's supernatural powers culminated with the discovery of the saint's supposed tongue when three centuries later his tomb was opened and a piece of reddened tissue fell out of his skull.

2.8.4 The cult

The figure of Saint John of Nepomuk is often encountered in Central Europe, including the Czech Republic, Italy, Germany, Poland and Lithuania, rarely Ukraine. He is usually portrayed with a halo of five stars, commemorating the stars that hovered over the Vltava River on the night of his murder. Other attributes useful to identify his pictures are: a priestly dress, the palm of martyrs, carrying a cross, an angel indicating silence by a finger over the lips. His tomb, a Baroque monument cast in silver and silver-gilt that was designed by Fischer von Erlach, stands in St Vitus Cathedral, Prague. A statue of Saint John of Nepomuk has often been erected on bridges in many countries, such as on the Ponte Milvio in Rome. There is also a commemorative plaque on a bridge leading out of Obergurgl, Austria depicting Nepomuk holding a finger to his lips, as if protecting a secret.

2.8.5 Music

John of Nepomuk mass in G-major [11] by Gerald Spitzner.

2.8.6 Notes

[1] Krčmář, Mgr. Luděk. "Saint John of Nepomuk". SJN.cz. If in 1369 John of Pomuk was a notary public, he must have been more than twenty years old. Thus he was probably born sometimes between 1340 and 1350 [1349].

[2] Pubitschka, Gesch., IV, app.; Pelzel ed., "Geschichte König Wenzels", I: "Urkundenbuch", 143-63

[3] l'ed. Stenzel in "Scrittura. il rerum Silesiacarum", I, 1835, pp. 213 sqq.

[4] Archiv für österreichische Geschichte, LX, 1880, pp. 418 sq.

[5] "Scriptores rerum Prussicarum", III, Leipzig 1860 -, 87

[6] cf. Schmude in "Zeitschrift für kathol. Theologie", 1883, 90 sqq.

[7] *St. John of Nepomuk* official website, SJN.cz

[8] The first queen was Johanna of Bavaria; the second one was her cousin Sofia of Bavaria.

[9] *Kronika česká*, first printed in Bohemian, Prague 1541; then translated in German and after two centuries also in Latin by Gelasius Dobner (6 volumes., Prague, 1761-83).

[10] Bohuslav Balbinus. *Vita beati Joannis Nepomuceni martyris*, Praga, 1670; It was reprinted in the Bollandists' *Acta sanctorum* III, May, pp 668-80.

[11] "Johannes Nepomuk Messe in G-Dur" (in German).

2.8.7 See also

Pilgrimage Church of Saint John of Nepomuk

2.8.8 External links

- The "official" page of John of Nepomuk

- *Catholic Encyclopedia* (1910): "St. John Nepomucene" This provides a Catholic point of view

- *Christian Classics Ethereal Library at Calvin College: "John of Nepomuk"* This provides a Protestant point of view. It was also the source of the initial version of this article.

- Chisholm, Hugh, ed. (1911). "Nepomuk, John of". *Encyclopædia Britannica* (11th ed.). Cambridge University Press.

- Zdarns.cz

- St. John Nepomuk, Martyr at the Christian Iconography web site

2.9 Philip Weiss

Philip Weiss is an American journalist who co-edits *Mondoweiss* ("a news website devoted to covering American foreign policy in the Middle East, chiefly from a progressive Jewish perspective"[3]) with journalist Adam Horowitz.[3][4] Weiss describes himself as an anti-Zionist and rejects the label "post-Zionist."[5]

2.9.1 Career

Weiss is the author of the novel *Cock-a-Doodle-Doo* (1996)[6] and the non-fiction book *American Taboo: A Murder In The Peace Corps* (2004).[7] He co-edited *The Goldstone Report: The Legacy of the Landmark Investigation of the Gaza Conflict* (2011) with Adam Horowitz and Lizzy Ratner.[8]

Weiss has written for *New York* magazine,[9] *Harper's Magazine,*[10] *Esquire*, and the *New York Observer*.[11][12]

In 2006 he began writing a daily blog called *Mondoweiss* on *The New York Observer* website which began to focus only on "Jewish issues" like "the Iraq disaster and my Jewishness, Zionism, neo-conservatism, Israel, Palestine." In the spring of 2007 he started *Mondoweiss* as an independent blog.[13][14]

2.9.2 Books

- 2011: *The Goldstone Report: The Legacy of the Landmark Investigation of the Gaza Conflict*, by Adam Horowitz, Lizzy Ratner, Philip Weiss, Naomi Klein, et al.[15]

- 2004: *American Taboo: A Murder In The Peace Corps*[16][17]

- 1996: *Cock-a-Doodle-Doo*[1]

2.9.3 References

[1] "Cool Cynic: Philip Weiss". *Entertainment Weekly*. 30 June 1995.

[2] "Mondo Weiss". *Tablet*. 20 January 2011.

[3] About: Mondowiess

[4] Phil Weiss at *Mondoweiss*.

[5] Philip Weiss, "I'm gonna wave my freak flag high (why I say I'm an 'Anti-Zionist,' not a 'Post-Zionist')", Mondoweiss blog, January 10, 2009.

[6] Philip Weiss, *Cock-a-Doodle-Doo*, St. Martin's Press, March 1996, ISBN 0312141009 ISBN 978-0312141004

[7] Publisher Harper Collins web page on Philip Weiss, *American Taboo: A Murder In The Peace Corps*, 2004.

[8] Philip Weiss, Adam Horowitz, Lizzy Ratner, *The Goldstone Report: The Legacy of the Landmark Investigation of the Gaza Conflict*, Nation Books , January 11, 2011, ISBN 1568586418 ISBN 978-1568586410

[9] Philip Weiss at *New York Magazine*.

[10] Philip Weiss at *Harper's Magazine*.

[11] Biography from Harper Collins

[12] Philip Weiss at *New York Observer*.

[13] Adas, Jane.   "From The Link's Links - http://www. mondoweiss.net," *The Link,* Vol. 43, Issue 1, Americans for Middle East Understanding, January - March 2010:12.

[14] Philip Weiss, Blogging about Israel and Jewish identity raises Observer hackles, *The American Conservative*, June 4, 2007.

[15] *Publisher's Weekly* review

[16] Bob Shacochis, Nonfiction: "American Taboo" by Philip Weiss Review of *American Taboo* Salon.com, July 20, 2004.

[17] Peter Godwin, "A Cold Case". Review of *American Taboo* in *The New York Times Book Review*, June 27, 2004.

2.9.4 Further reading

- Adas, Jane.   "From The Link's Links - http://www.mondoweiss.net," *The Link,* Vol. 43, Issue 1, Americans for Middle East Understanding, January - March 2010:12.

- PBS. "Extended Interviews: American Jews and Israel - Philip Weiss, writer and blogger," *PBS*, June 12, 2009.

- Philip Weiss: A Jewish Argument around the Arab Revolt at Radio Open Source

2.9.5 External links

- Appearances on C-SPAN

2.10   Richard McCaslin

The **Phantom Patriot** was the name taken by Richard McCaslin[1] of Carson City, Nevada, who, on January 19, 2002, attempted an attack on the Bohemian Grove.[2] He was imprisoned in California. He is the subject of the song "Phantom Patriot" by Les Claypool on his album *Of Whales and Woe*.[3]

2.10.1   Background

McCaslin, wearing a skull mask and a blue jumpsuit with "Phantom Patriot" written in red on his chest, infiltrated the site of Bohemian Grove, just north of San Francisco. He was heavily armed with "a [pump-action/shotgun hybrid, a .45 caliber handgun, a crossbow, a 2-foot-long sword, a knife and a fireworks mortar tube." McCaslin slept in one of the cabins overnight. The following morning, he found the 30 ft. owl statue, then later encountered caretaker, Fred Yeager and maintenance man, Bob Hipkiss.[4] McCaslin set a fire in the empty banquet hall, then was later removed peacefully by local law enforcement officers and was briefly held at the mental health ward of the Sonoma County Jail. He later claimed to have seen the documentary,"Dark Secrets Inside Bohemian Grove" by talk show host Alex Jones.[5]

2.10.2   After prison release

McCaslin was paroled on 19 May 2008. On June 28, 2011, McCaslin (using the name "Thoughtcrime") protested outside the Alcoa plant in Davenport, Iowa where President Barack Obama was speaking. He accused Obama (as well as the Bushs, the Clintons and others) of being a [reptoid/human hybrid,or "blue blood."[6]

Most recently, McCaslin has adopted Las Vegas, Nevada as his base of operations. His story appears in the 2013 book, "Heroes in the Night; Inside the Real Life Superhero Movement" by Tea Krulos.[7] He also has three Phantom Patriot videos on YouTube.

2.10.3 References

[1] Krulos, T. (2013). *Heroes in the Night: Inside the Real Life Superhero Movement*. Chicago Review Press, Incorporated. ISBN 978-1-61374-775-9. Retrieved 8 April 2015. p.55.

[2] Masked man enters, attacks Bohemian Grove:'Phantom' expected armed resistance, by Peter Fimrite, *San Francisco Chronicle*, January 24, 2002

[3] "Les Claypool - Discography - Les Claypool". *lesclaypool.com*. Retrieved 8 April 2015.

[4] Bohemian Grove intruder says he feared human sacrifices, *Illuminati Conspiracy Archive*

[5] Bohemian Grove commando found guilty, *SFGate*, April 17, 2002

[6] Rashah McChesney. Alcoa protester believes Obama is an alien, *Quad-City Times*

[7] Krulos, T. (2013). *Heroes in the Night: Inside the Real Life Superhero Movement*. Chicago Review Press, Incorporated. ISBN 978-1-61374-775-9. Retrieved 8 April 2015.

2.11 Sara Jane Lippincott

Lippincott's house in New Brighton

Sara Jane Lippincott (1823–1904) was better known by the pseudonym **Grace Greenwood**. She was an American author, poet, and lecturer. One of the first women to gain access into the Congressional press galleries, she used her questions to advocate for social reform and women's rights.

2.11.1 Biography

Sara Jane Lippincott, circa 1850

Sara Jane Clarke was born on September 23, 1823 at Pompey, New York to parents Deborah Baker Clarke (c. 1791–1881) and Dr. Thaddeus C. Clarke (1770–1854).[1] Her family moved to New Brighton, Pennsylvania, where her father practiced as a physician. There she attended the Greenwood Institute, a ladies' academy, from which she may have taken her pseudonym. On October 17, 1853 she married Leander K. Lippincott, and they had a daughter, Annie Grace, born October 3, 1855. Her husband left the country in 1876 after indictment for land fraud. Later she lived with her daughter in New Rochelle, New York, where she died of bronchitis[2] on April 20, 1904. Grace Greenwood is buried in the Civil War section of Grove Cemetery in New Brighton.[3]

Career

Grace Greenwood's earliest writing was poetry and children's stories, which she published in local papers. In 1844, she drew national attention, at age 21, with a poem published in the *New York Mirror*. She wrote under both her given name and her pseudonym. In the February 14, 1846 issue of the *Home Journal*, *The Wife's Appeal*, a poem by Miss Sara J. Clarke, is published just above *Tit-for-Tat*, a story by Grace Greenwood. Her work was published frequently in the widely read magazines of the day. Her poetry received significant critical attention. She became a prominent member of the literary society of New York along with Anne Lynch Botta, Edgar Allan Poe, Margaret Fuller, Ralph Waldo Emerson and Horace Greeley, Richard Henry Stoddard, Andrew Carnegie, Mary Mapes Dodge, Julia Ward Howe, Charles Butler, Fitz-Greene Halleck, Delia Bacon, and Bayard Taylor, among others. By October 1849, *Godey's Lady's Book* listed her as an assistant editor and she was also editor of *Godey's Dollar Newspaper*. Her published collection *Poems* (1851) included passionate poetry and references to her intimate friendship to Anna Phillips, indicating an acceptance of intimate same sex friendships.[3]

She became a highly respected journalist and consistently argued for the reform of women's roles and rights.[4] In 1852, she went to Europe on an assignment for the *New York Times*. Greenwood was the first woman reporter on the *Times* payroll.[5] She joined the *National Era*, a weekly abolitionist newspaper, and copy edited the serialized original version of Harriet Beecher Stowe's *Uncle Tom's Cabin* as well as writing columns, travel letters, and articles. Her staunch abolitionist views contributed to the ongoing national controversy. Nathaniel Hawthorne criticized her travel letters, calling her an "ink-stained woman" and claiming he could do as well. Despite this, Greenwood seems to have gotten along amiably with Hawthorne's family. She dedicated her children's book *Recollections of My Childhood, and Other Stories* to Julian and Una Hawthorne. She also became a correspondent for the *Saturday Evening Post*.

The Little Pilgrim *masthead, 1855*

In 1853, Greenwood and her husband started *The Little Pilgrim*,[6] an American children's magazine. She was soon producing magazine articles and essays. After her husband

fled the United States in 1876 to escape prosecution for misappropriation of government funds, Greenwood continued her writing and resumed lecturing in order to support herself and her daughter.[3]

Greenwood lectured extensively before and during the Civil War, giving particular attention to her abolitionist stance and to other social issues, such as prison and asylum reform, and the abolition of capital punishment. President Abraham Lincoln referred to her as "Grace Greenwood the Patriot".[2] However, women's rights became the focus of her speeches, particularly after the war. Her writings from this period were republished in *Records of Five Years* (1867). By the 1870s, Greenwood wrote primarily for the *New York Times*. Her articles focused mainly on women's issues, such as advocating for Fanny Kemble's right to wear trousers, Susan B. Anthony's right to vote and all women's right to receive equal pay for equal work.

Greenwood and her daughter moved to Europe around 1882. She worked for the *London Journal*, and also wrote a biography, *Queen Victoria: Her Girlhood and Womanhood* (1883). In 1887 she returned to the United States and continued to work until 1900. Her obituary was on the front page of the *New York Times*, "proving her importance as a literary figure in the nineteenth century".[3]

2.11.2   Works

- *Greenwood Leaves* (1850)

- *History of my Pets* (1851)

- *Poems* (1851)

- *Recollections of my Childhood, and other stories* (1852)

- *Haps and Mishaps of a Tour in Europe* (1854)

- *Merrie England* (1855)

- *Forest Tragedy, and other tales* (1856)

- *Stories and Legends of Travel and History* (1857)

- *Stories from Famous Ballads* (1860)

- *Bonnie Scotland* (1861)

- *Records of Five Years* (1867)

- *Stories and Sights of France and Italy* (1867)

- *Stories of Many Lands* (1867)

- *Summer Etchings in Colorado* (1873)

- *New Life in New Lands* (1873)

- *Heads and Tails: studies and stories of pets* (1875)

- *Emma Abbott, prima donna* (1878)

- *Queen Victoria, her girlhood and womanhood* (1883)

- *Stories for Home-folks, young and old* (1884)

- *Stories and Sketches* (1892) (with Rossiter W. Raymond)

- *Treasures from Fairyland* (1879)

2.11.3 References

[1] "Beaver County History Online". *Sara Jane Clarke (Grace Greenwood)*. Retrieved January 31, 2008.

[2] "Portraits of American Women Writers". *GRACE GREENWOOD (1823-1904)*. Retrieved January 31, 2008.

[3] "English Literature: Nineteenth Century: Authors: Greenwood, Grace (1823-1904)". *Literature Online*. Retrieved January 31, 2008.(requires interlibrary account access)

[4] Garrett, Paula K. "A Splinter Off the" Sound Old Theological Block": Grace Greenwood's Humorous Revision of the American Jeremiad." Studies in American Humor (2005): 17-43.

[5] "New York State Newspapers". *The New York Times : A Chronology: 1851-2006*. Retrieved February 2, 2008.

[6] "American children's periodicals, 1789-1872". *The Little Pilgrim ; Oct 1853-Dec 1868*. Retrieved February 1, 2008.

2.11.4 External links

- Works by Grace Greenwood at Project Gutenberg

- Works by or about Grace Greenwood at Internet Archive

- Works by Grace Greenwood at LibriVox (public domain audiobooks)

2.12 Significant Others (novel)

Significant Others (1987) is the fifth book in the *Tales of the City* series by American novelist Armistead Maupin. It originally was serialized in the *San Francisco Examiner*.

2.12.1 Plot summary

It is now 1985 and much of the action is set in the Russian River area north of San Francisco. Here, successful businessmen from around the globe gather at Bohemian Grove for a three-week encampment of male bonding, while downriver from them events at Wimminwood, a lesbian music and arts festival, threaten the relationship of DeDe Halcyon-Day and D'orothea Wilson.

Returning characters include Mary Ann Singleton, who is having difficulty balancing her commitment to her career as a local talk show hostess with her obligations as a wife to Brian and mother to Shawna, the child of her friend Connie, who entrusted the girl's care to Mary Ann on her deathbed; Michael Tolliver, the romantic gay man who has tested HIV-positive and is taking AZT to combat the threat to his immune system; and Anna Madrigal, the transgender landlady who mothers her tenants at 28 Barbary Lane on Russian Hill and is fighting to preserve the historic wooden steps of the lane.

New characters include Thack Sweeney, who meets Michael during a tour of Alcatraz and Wren Douglas, a plus-size model whose best-selling self-help book offers hope to overweight women. There is also a focus on a previously minor character, Roger "Booter" Manigault, DeDe's stepfather and a member of the Bohemian Club, who accidentally stumbles into Wimminwood and is held captive by one of its more militant organizers. Brian's college-aged nephew Jed also makes an appearance as a young Reaganite more interested in getting into Harvard Law and making money than having fun.

2.13 The Family (club)

The Family is a private club in San Francisco, California, formed in 1901 by newspapermen who left the Bohemian Club. The club maintains a clubhouse in the city as well as rural property 35 miles to the south in Woodside.

An exclusive, invitation only, all-male club, it calls new members "Babies", regular members "Children" and the club president "Father". The club rules forbid the use of its facilities or services for the purposes of trade or business. Furthermore, each member must certify that he will not deduct any part of club payments as business expenses for federal or state income tax purposes. The Family sponsors charity projects such as a hospital in Guatemala.[1]

2.13.1 History

The Bohemian Club was formed by and for journalists, and included a number who worked for the *San Fran-*

Entrance to 545 Powell, San Francisco, showing a design etched in glass: a large bird and its four babies in a nest, surrounded by a buckled belt that reads "The Family ·· Keep Young ··"

cisco *Examiner* and other papers owned by William Randolph Hearst. In 1901, Ambrose Bierce wrote a poem that seemed to predict or even call for President William McKinley's death by an assassin's bullet, and the Hearst chain ran the piece. When McKinley was assassinated shortly thereafter, opponents of Hearst created a fervour over the poem's publication, ending Hearst's ambitions for the US presidency and causing the Hearst newsmen to resign from the Bohemian Club in protest over the Bohemian Club's banning of Hearst newspapers from the premises. A group of 14 reporters, editors, and other resigned members formed their own club and called it "The Family".[2]

Early public activities by the club included the sponsoring of a horse race called the "Family Club Handicap" held in Oakland in 1904. A racehorse named "Fossil" took first place, receiving a silver cup from the Family as well as US$1,000 from the California Jockey Club.[3]

The Family clubhouse was originally located at 228 Post Street, but the building was lost two days after the 1906 San Francisco earthquake in the subsequent calamitous fire, though not before serving as temporary rest station and meal place for earthquake victims such as the bereft Conreid Metropolitan Opera Company.[4] The club rebuilt at

the corner of Powell and Bush Streets, and still conducts meetings at this site two blocks from the peak of Nob Hill.

The Family's clubhouse has served as a venue for musical events such as an annual benefit for San Francisco Sinfonietta[5] as well as black-tie dinner lectures by various experts and personages such as Stanlee Gatti speaking to benefit horticultural programs[6] and Charles M. Schulz appearing to promote the Cartoon Art Museum.[7]

2.13.2 The Family Farm

The Family conducts annual social events among the redwood and oak trees and open meadows at its rural property on the San Francisco peninsula. The Family Farm entrance is at 1400 Portola Road in Woodside.

In 1909, Family club members decided upon the Woodside location for their rural getaways. While summering there in 1912, club members of a variety of religious backgrounds including Judaism, Protestantism and Catholicism pooled their resources to build a Catholic church in nearby Portola Valley: Our Lady of the Wayside Church. Architect member James R. Miller assigned the design of the church to a promising young draftsman at his firm, Timothy L. Pflueger. This was Pflueger's first architectural commission, and was the start of his interaction with the Family. Pflueger would soon join the Family to become a member in good standing.[2]

An annual "Flight Play", as well as a number of other stage and musical performances, are written and performed by club members. Plays aren't published or performed beyond the privacy of the club, and all original written materials are the sole property of the Club.[8] One handwritten musical score, *Thine Enemy*, composed by Meredith Willson for the 1937 Flight Play 20 years before *The Music Man* was staged on Broadway, will be donated by The Family to a museum in the composer's birthplace, Mason City, Iowa.[9] Diego Rivera and José Clemente Orozco were guests of Timothy Pflueger's at the Farm in 1930. The two leftist Mexican muralists argued forcefully with one another about art during one visit.[10]

2.13.3 Famous members

- General of the Army and General of the Air Force Henry "Hap" Arnold

- Edward Bowes, realtor[11]

- Ty Cobb, famous baseball player

- Colbert Coldwell, founder of Coldwell Banker[12]

- Henry J. Crocker, nephew of Charles Crocker, banker, oil magnate, 1903 mayoral candidate, member of the Committee of Fifty (1906)[11]

- Arthur Fiedler, conductor

- Herbert Fleishhacker, businessman, civic leader, philanthropist[11]

- John Emmett Gerrity, California modernist artist[10]

- Henry F. Grady, First US Ambassador to India; Dean of the Commerce department at the University of California, Berkeley; President of American President Lines

- Peter E. Haas, Levi-Strauss executive, son of Walter A. Haas[13]

- William Randolph Hearst, newspaper publisher

- Herbert Hoover, President of the United States

- Joseph M. Long, founder of Longs Drugs

- Clarence W. W. Mayhew, architect[14]

- James Rupert Miller, architect[2]

- General of the Armies John J. Pershing

- Timothy Pflueger, architect[15]

- William Saroyan, author and dramatist

- Colonel Charles Stanton, Pershing's Chief of Staff

- George Sterling, poet and playwright[16]

- Max Thelen, senior partner at Thelen LLP

- Henry Albert van Coenen Torchiana, author, Consul-General from the Netherlands and Commissioner of the Panama-Pacific International Exposition[17]

- Meredith Willson, American composer, lyricist, Broadway producer

2.13.4   See also

- List of American gentlemen's clubs

- Olympic Club

- Pacific-Union Club

2.13.5   References

[1] SFGate. *The Chosen Few: S.F.'s exclusive clubs carry on traditions of fellowship, culture – and discrimination.* Adair Lara. July 18, 2004.

[2] Poletti, Therese; Tom Paiva (2008). *Art Deco San Francisco: The Architecture of Timothy Pflueger.* Princeton Architectural Press. ISBN 1-56898-756-0.

[3] New York Times. December 11, 1904. *Fossil Won Family Club Handicap.*

[4] Calisphere. University of California. Ernest Goerlitz. *Story of the San Francisco earthquake and conflagration as far as it affected the Conreid Metropolitan Opera Company April 18th, 19th and 20th, 1906.*

[5] SF Sinfonietta. Events calendar

[6] SFGate. *Benefits: Elton John to rock first Bridge School gala.* Catherine Bigelow. October 22, 2006.

[7] Animation World Network. *Chow Down With Charles M. Schulz.* July 12, 1996.

[8] American Association for the Advancement of Science, Pacific Coast Committee (1915). *Nature and Science on the Pacific Coast.* P. Elder. p. 258.

[9] Globe Gazette, February 17, 2007. John Skipper, " 'The Family' plans to bring original Willson score home." Retrieved on August 15, 2009.

[10] Smithsonian. Archives of American Art. Research Collections, Oral History Interviews. *John Emmett Gerrity interview, 1965 Jan. 20*

[11] San Francisco Genealogy. The Family Club. *1905 Officers and Members*

[12] Rootsweb Genealogy. Ancestry. *Colbert Coldwell*

[13] Berkeley Alumni. *California* magazine, March/April 2007. Sather Gate. Keeping in Touch. *1940.*

[14] ArchitectDB. *Clarence Mayhew*

[15] Timothy Pflueger letters. Undated, received from Diego Rivera.

[16] "Sterling a poet? Read wife's charges in divorce plea." San Francisco Call, December 16, 1913. Part 2, page 9.

[17] Calisphere. University of California. *Dinner by H. Van Boenen Torchiana, Commissioner from Netherlands*

2.14 The Secret Rulers of the World

The Secret Rulers of the World is a five-part documentary series, produced by World of Wonder Productions and written, directed by, and featuring Jon Ronson. The series was first shown on Channel 4 in April and May 2001. The series details Ronson's encounters with conspiracy theorists. It accompanies Ronson's book *Them: Adventures with Extremists*, which covers similar topics and describes many of the same events.

2.14.1 Part 1: *The Legend of Ruby Ridge*

Original air date: 29 April 2001

Jon Ronson meets with Randy Weaver and daughter Rachel, two of the surviving members of the Weaver family. The film shows previously unseen archive footage to describe the life of a family who claim to have moved to a cabin in Ruby Ridge, Idaho, to live peacefully, and escape what they saw as the tyrannical elite of international bankers bent on enslaving the world. Ronson also explains how the Weaver family's conspiracy theories became a shocking tragedy when the American Government killed two of the family members, their dog, and shot and wounded Randy Weaver and Kevin Harris, whom the Weaver family considered their son. Ronson explores the unsympathetic media response to the killings and how this incident might have influenced the siege at Waco, the Oklahoma City bombing, and the growth of the American militia movement.

2.14.2 Part 2: *David Icke, The Lizards and The Jews*

Original air date: 6 May 2001

Jon Ronson follows David Icke as he promotes his theory that "the elite are genetically descended from a race of 12-foot, blood-drinking, shape-shifting lizards". During the film Icke is accused by a leftist protest group in Canada of antisemitism. The documentary explores the theme of whether Icke literally means lizards — as he steadfastly maintains — or whether the reptilians are a coded reference to Jews, which Icke denies vehemently. Ronson concludes that Icke is probably not an anti-Semite, and comes to have misgivings about the Icke protesters' methods and their attempts to silence Icke.

See also: Reptilians

2.14.3 Part 3: *Timothy McVeigh, The Oklahoma Bomber*

Original air date: 13 May 2001

Before his involvement in the Oklahoma City bombing, Timothy McVeigh believed that a shadowy elite secretly controlled the governments of the world, conspiring to establish a genocidal New World Order. He believed that the Alfred P. Murrah building was local New World Order headquarters. But many other theorists are convinced that the world only knows part of an apparent complex conspiracy story behind the bombing. Ronson meets a number of theorists whilst investigating the story, and concludes his film in Elohim City, a private Christian Identity movement compound in Oklahoma.

2.14.4 Part 4: *The Satanic Shadowy Elite?*

Original air date: 20 May 2001

Jon Ronson follows conspiracy theorist and radio host Alex Jones as he attempts to infiltrate the annual gathering of dignitaries and business leaders (reportedly including George Bush and Henry Kissinger) at the Bohemian Grove. The film includes footage of attendees dressed in robes and burning an effigy at the foot of a giant stone owl. Jones believes that the ceremony is related to occult secret societies. After the event, Ronson meets comedy actor and fellow attendee Harry Shearer who describes the event as a glorified fraternity party. Shearer largely dismisses Jones's dramatic retelling of the gathering and notes that the music is supplied by The Symphony Orchestra of San Francisco.

2.14.5 Part 5: *The Bilderberg Group*

Original air date: 27 May 2001

Ronson teams up with reporter James P. Tucker, Jr., who has been investigating the Bilderberg Group, an annual invitation-only conference, for over thirty years. According to Tucker, around 130 guests, most of whom are persons of influence in business, academic, or political circles, meet annually in secret. The duo encounter unwelcoming suited security men and a car chase. Ronson also interviews Group founder Denis Healey.

2.14.6 References

2.14.7 External links

- *The Secret Rulers of the World* at the Internet Movie Database

Chapter 3

Text and image sources, contributors, and licenses

3.1 Text

- **Bohemian Grove** *Source:* https://en.wikipedia.org/wiki/Bohemian_Grove?oldid=684623011 *Contributors:* AxelBoldt, Mav, Ed Poor, Zoe, Hephaestos, Michael Hardy, Llywrch, Jschrempp, Ronabop, Darkwind, Cimon Avaro, Oliver Crow, Jengod, Ventura, Daniel Quinlan, WhisperToMe, Wik, Nv8200pa, Khranus, AnonMoos, Jamesday, Damion, RedWolf, Mirv, Wjhonson, Merovingian, Eggz, Mushroom, GreatWhiteNortherner, Dina, Carnildo, DocWatson42, Geeoharee, Tom harrison, Orangemike, Obli, Mackerm, Bobblewik, Sexyfoxboy, Geni, Mr d logan, Cwirtanen, RetiredUser2, Eanschuessler, Gary D, The stuart, D6, Rich Farmbrough, Eric Shalov, Mt2131, Moulding, Mairi, Boho, Kine, Bobo192, Infocidal, Viriditas, Justinsomnia, RussBlau, Zachlipton, Alansohn, Uncle.bungle, Arthena, Punarbhava, SlimVirgin, Zsero, Plasma tornadoes, Hierarchypedia, Mikeo, Bsadowski1, Crosbiesmith, Sburke, Arnomane, Bbatsell, Arwcheek, Striver, GregorB, Black-cats, Rchamberlain, Male1979, Matthew Platts, Toussaint, Silverwood, Kbdank71, RxS, ConradKilroy, Rjwilmsi, Koavf, TheRingess, MZM-cBride, Wingover, Durin, G Clark, AJR, Jrtayloriv, Vidkun, GangofOne, YurikBot, Peter G Werner, RussBot, Hydrargyrum, Gaius Cornelius, Thane, Wiki alf, Chick Bowen, Bloodofox, Harrisale, GeorgeC, Blenda Lovelace, FluxFuser, Halloween jack, Bruce Hall, Avraham, Tuck-erresearch, Abune, JLaTondre, DoriSmith, Jonathan.s.kt, Demigod of the Old Testament, SmackBot, Classicfilms, KnowledgeOfSelf, J-beda, JJay, Edgar181, Xaosflux, KennethJ, Ghosts&empties, Betacommand, Nfgii, ERcheck, Chris the speller, Bluebot, Achmelvic, Jprg1966, Re-named user Sloane, Ctbolt, Zachorious, Anabus, Chendy, Muboshgu, Brimba, OrphanBot, KevM, Decidus, Dreadstar, BullRangifer, Jkalani, Risker, Coconuteire, Ohconfucius, Will Beback, The Ungovernable Force, Esrever, ManiacK, Sir Nicholas de Mimsy-Porpington, JoshuaZ, Nyg-dan, Arbustoo, A. Parrot, Mr Stephen, Meco, TastyPoutine, Midnightblueowl, Wvoutlaw2002, Dr.K., Chris Stangl, JoeBot, Jamesflanagan99, Zero sharp, Tony Fox, QuantumOne, Saintlink, George100, J Milburn, Wikipediareader, Dycedarg, Location, Kitten b, ElectricEye, Cydebot, Zac Stewart, Epbr123, Wikid77, Dubc0724, Daniel, Barnej, Oliver202, Marek69, Missvain, John254, Lajsikonik, KevinWho, AntiVandalBot, Yonatan, Dekkanar, Rambone, Blue Tie, Midnightmuse, Prolog, Tchoutoye, Dr who1975, Drewk, NSH001, Alphachimpbot, Hoponpop69, Rubensni, Radrik, RJFerret, Husond, LLM68, Caribou58, MER-C, Max Hyre, Roleplayer, Jmisraje, VoABot II, MartinDK, QuizzicalBee, Jllm06, Bradrules, Lenschulwitz, MetsBot, Prester John, Glen, Turtlens, GuelphGryphon98, Glp~enwiki, Grandia01, Kateshortforbob, J.delanoy, Captain panda, Bapho~enwiki, Munkachy, Reedy Bot, McSly, Wiz-Pro3, Vanished user g454XxNpUVWvxzlr, DadaNeem, Whoblitzell, Robert-greer, MetsFan76, 2help, Acidskater, Bricology, Xiahou, That-Vela-Fella, Thedjatclubrock, Esparza74, Indubitably, Philip Trueman, TXiKi-BoT, Oshwah, Tom612pl, Tomkara, Gg1234, Wolfraem, Mkubica, Ksandoe, Sicjedi, TravelingCat, SteinAlive, LB48Steve03, Rontrigger, Vital-Drop, Neobob187, Zenlax, Kfc1864, Spartan, Twoshedds, Bentogoa, Qst, Ajbaer5, Damian Thorne, Lightmouse, CeruleanFilms, NastalgicCam, Mblaxill, ImageRemovalBot, Elassint, Youpilot, ClueBot, Binksternet, PipepBot, EoGuy, Arkalochori, Eightnine, Bohemiangrove740, Trivial-ist, Excirial, John Nevard, GobblinKing, Mkneuer, Morel, Stepheng3, Yolodave, Aitias, DumZiBoT, XLinkBot, AgnosticPreachersKid, Rror, Ost316, Critical Chris, Good Olfactory, Drolz09, Freddy Conzals, NCDane, Addbot, Researchwatch, TomKWS, Fieldday-sunday, Vishnava, Download, Ahmad2099, Glane23, Kyle1278, Doniago, Buzzme2h3aven35, Tide rolls, Lightbot, Stevenspecht, Yadin137, Jarble, LuK3, Swarm, Luckas-bot, Tohd8BohaithuGh1, Fraggle81, Freedomjusticepeace, AnomieBOT, Mike Hayes, Krelnik, Jim1138, RandomAct, Williamsburg-land, Tokyotown8, Gy57f37gjh59gj, XxIblisxx, Grim23, Jmundo, Patriot2522, Tyrol5, FrescoBot, METAK RAMAH, Blackguard SF, Annexa-tious, DivineAlpha, PrincessofLlyr, Jonesey95, ImageTagBot, Skyerise, Thewatchdog2012, Trappist the monk, Lotje, Harrysstupid, Arcadia616, RjwilmsiBot, Beyond My Ken, Kiko4564, User2112, QuantumGnome, Jforsayeth, SlanderingWiki, K6ka, Itabletboy, ZéroBot, John Cline, Fæ, Bobbyswhirled, Ὁ οἶστρος, SporkBot, Rostz, Donner60, ChuispastonBot, ClueBot NG, Lhimec, Name Omitted, Jdperkins, Widr, Helpful Pixie Bot, Novusuna, Titodutta, Neptune's Trident, Annuitcoeptus, Hodeken, Townsaiso, Northamerica1000, Sailingfanblues, Yosesphdaviyd, Odessious, PaintedCarpet, DaylightWasting, W.D., Codeh, Hmainsbot1, Thenewguy34, Ne Ne14fun, Aronk123, KILLuminati33, Nimetapoeg, Fycafterpro, Destroman2, Julian Felsenburgh, GWBushism, Grapestomper9, Dozei, WPGA2345, Jamez1502, Monkbot, Fyddlestix, Chronos-tat, LivingSelfSufficient, Distancesarewhite, Iwilsonp, Prinsgezinde, Peter Anastopulos and Anonymous: 538

- **Henry Edwards (entomologist)** *Source:* https://en.wikipedia.org/wiki/Henry_Edwards_(entomologist)?oldid=659568539 *Contributors:* Jimf-bleak, WhisperToMe, Tpbradbury, Rich Farmbrough, FeanorStar7, Rjwilmsi, Koavf, RussBot, Gaius Cornelius, SmackBot, Brianyoumans, Notafly, Chris the speller, Ohconfucius, BrownHairedGirl, Disavian, SandyGeorgia, Dl2000, Ssilvers, TonyTheTiger, Marek69, DShamen, MER-C, Maias, Lasius, Connormah, WolfmanSF, CommonsDelinker, DrKay, Aboutmovies, Fainites, GimmeBot, Bfpage, Ealdgyth, Maralia, Efe, Sfan00 IMG, Binksternet, Icarusgeek, Jappalang, P. S. Burton, NuclearWarfare, Laser brain, Dthomsen8, Rreagan007, Addbot, Yobot,

63

Materialscientist, Tbhotch, RjwilmsiBot, Andreas Philopater, Wikipelli, Jsayre64, ClueBot NG, Sharktopus, Dr. Whooves, DaylightWasting, Aranea Mortem, Temperingking, Zacharydodd, Bobpop23, Garrettandhunter23, BattyBot, LaurentianShield, Monkbot, KasparBot and Anonymous: 21

- **Bohemian Club** *Source:* https://en.wikipedia.org/wiki/Bohemian_Club?oldid=675580119 *Contributors:* Espen, The Anome, Jschrempp, Ahoerstemeier, RodC, WhisperToMe, Goethean, Postdlf, Ashley Y, Mushroom, DocWatson42, Tom harrison, Varlaam, Sexyfoxboy, Cwirtanen, Maikel, Rich Farmbrough, Bender235, CanisRufus, RoyBoy, Boho, Walkiped, Zsero, BaronLarf, Hierarchypedia, Grenavitar, Gavin86, Tabletop, SDC, Kralizec!, Ashmoo, Grammarbot, Tim!, Rogerd, TheRingess, Heah, Vegaswikian, FlaBot, Gwernol, YurikBot, Wavelength, Gaius Cornelius, Wiki alf, Clashfrankcastle, JTM, Malcolma, MSJapan, Gilemon, Syd Midnight, SMcCandlish, DoriSmith, Jonathan.s.kt, Kiwifilm, SmackBot, Impaciente, J-beda, Bwithh, JJay, Kintetsubuffalo, Xaosflux, ERcheck, Bluebot, Renamed user Sloane, Brimba, Zambaccian, Radagast83, Breadandroses, Bdushaw, Anlace, Robofish, Nygdan, Perrylok, Noah Salzman, Meco, Quaeler, Twas Now, QuantumOne, Daisy arkansas, BeenAroundAWhile, Jordan Brown, Bellerophon5685, Koans, Technogreek43, Missvain, Dr who1975, Credema, 332uncletoby, Alphachimpbot, Desertsky85451, Magioladitis, Sofa jazz man, PEAR, Esalso, Prester John, Glen, Tgeairn, Enter the PHiL, Robertgreer, Bricology, Wikieditor06, Philip Trueman, Mercurywoodrose, Wikidemon, Semper7, Rockstone35, Oculi, Tacobellis, CeruleanFilms, Dillard421, Ahuitzotl, ClueBot, Binksternet, Trivialist, Skling1-13-97, XLinkBot, AgnosticPreachersKid, Ost316, Addbot, Poco a poco, Lestat44241, Rago, Luckas-bot, Fraggle81, Iambuilding7, AnomieBOT, Materialscientist, Tyrol5, FriscoKnight, Tim1357, Trappist the monk, RjwilmsiBot, Achilver, Jforsayeth, ZéroBot, Fullsailmu, Ὁ οἶστρος, ClueBot NG, Helpful Pixie Bot, Jadelink 6, Gurt Posh, Northamerica1000, Jcarterfan30, Clubwiki, DaylightWasting, ChrisGualtieri, Makecat-bot, Fox2k11, Melonkelon, Qwertygirl12 and Anonymous: 111

- **Cremation of Care** *Source:* https://en.wikipedia.org/wiki/Cremation_of_Care?oldid=662685446 *Contributors:* Michael Hardy, Mushroom, Tom harrison, Wyss, Khaosworks, Boho, Cmdrjameson, TheCoffee, Arnomane, Striver, Toussaint, Moonty, Harro5, JDoorjam, WiffleOrz, TruthTeller, DoriSmith, Jeffreymcmanus, Kiwifilm, JJay, Chris the speller, Renamed user Sloane, Kcordina, NicKK, Nygdan, Biruitorul, Drewk, Mtd2006, R'n'B, Mercurywoodrose, Sicjedi, Vexorg, Pepso2, Binksternet, Piledhigheranddeeper, Trivialist, John Nevard, Materialscientist, Citation bot, Pixiesdelight, Shwanzi, Ὁ οἶστρος, ClueBot NG, Helpful Pixie Bot, Frosty, Monkbot, Davidicus Disraeli and Anonymous: 39

- **List of Bohemian Club members** *Source:* https://en.wikipedia.org/wiki/List_of_Bohemian_Club_members?oldid=682942586 *Contributors:* The Cunctator, Koavf, Vegaswikian, Welsh, Nlu, Aboudaqn, RolandR, Ashrkfn, Collect, Wjenning, Eurodog, Cbuckley, Gondorian, Doug Weller, Nick Number, Mujokan, R'n'B, Laurusnobilis, Thomas.W, Rontrigger, Dusti, Pepso2, The Four Deuces, Binksternet, Niceguyedc, Trivialist, MarmadukePercy, Tassedethe, AnomieBOT, Jim1138, Emargie, Srich32977, Biograph1985, LittleWink, Mda3k, Erlynch, RRFW-Tommartin, Tylergrady8, Philippe (WMF), THATSBETTER, Yodabirdblue, AndyTheGrump, ClueBot NG, Bougnat87, Helpful Pixie Bot, Bwaldon4, Steeletrap, KlutchNeff, Monkbot and Anonymous: 51

- **List of Grove Plays** *Source:* https://en.wikipedia.org/wiki/List_of_Grove_Plays?oldid=686013980 *Contributors:* Davitf, Bearcat, Boho, BDD, Woohookitty, RadioFan, Pegship, DoriSmith, Classicfilms, Eurodog, Aristophanes68, Mack2, NSH001, R'n'B, Mercurywoodrose, Binksternet, Trivialist, Stepheng3, Tassedethe, Helpful Pixie Bot, Cetteferge, Jodosma, Monkbot and Anonymous: 3

- **Alex Jones (radio host)** *Source:* https://en.wikipedia.org/wiki/Alex_Jones_(radio_host)?oldid=685709602 *Contributors:* Zoe, Aaron, KF, Edward, Jimfbleak, William M. Connolley, Bueller 007, Vodex, Charles Matthews, PaulinSaudi, Dysprosia, Daniel Quinlan, WhisperToMe, Khranus, AnonMoos, Catskul, Bearcat, Dale Arnett, ZimZalaBim, Modulatum, Sam Spade, Wjhonson, Nach0king, Markewilliams, LGagnon, Caknuck, Isopropyl, ElBenevolente, Alan Liefting, Tom harrison, Boojit, MSGJ, Leflyman, Cool Hand Luke, Everyking, Bkonrad, Varlaam, Alexander.stohr, DO'Neil, Sexyfoxboy, Gyrofrog, Fishal, Geni, Popefauvexxiii, Skeeto, Antandrus, OverlordQ, SamClayton, JoJan, MisfitToys, Quarl, Oscar, Schwael, Rdsmith4, Tothebarricades.tk, JHCC, Sam, Klemen Kocjancic, Syvanen, Calwatch, Chmod007, The stuart, SYSS Mouse, PhotoBox, Mike Rosoft, Shiftchange, AliveFreeHappy, Discospinster, ElTyrant, Rich Farmbrough, Rhobite, Vsmith, User2004, MeltBanana, Antaeus Feldspar, ESkog, Kbh3rd, Narcisse, Project2501a, Mr. Billion, El C, Sourcecode, Lankiveil, Mwanner, Aude, Shanes, RoyBoy, Triona, Jpgordon, Ghostal~enwiki, Bobo192, John Vandenberg, Walkiped, Mrbill, Nihila, DragonGuyver, Polylerus, Pearle, Wayfarer, Geschichte, Papeschr, Alansohn, PaulHanson, Uncle.bungle, Eleland, Philip Cross, Philosophistry, Babajobu, JoaoRicardo, Riana, Calton, SlimVirgin, Hoary, Echuck215, DreamGuy, Wtmitchell, Velella, TaintedMustard, Fourthords, Zantastik, Danaman5, Lapinmies, Bnguyen, Dominic, Skyring, Bsadowski1, Arthur Warrington Thomas, Netkinetic, Ceyockey, Dismas, Stephen, Megan1967, OwenX, Woohookitty, Havermayer, Spettro9, Uncle G, BillC, MONGO, Bdj, Striver, KevinOKeeffe, Bluemoose, GregorB, LILVOKA, Blackcats, Male1979, Pictureuploader, RichardWeiss, Descendall, Cuchullain, BD2412, Kbdank71, Jclemens, Edison, RackAttack, Rjwilmsi, Nightscream, Koavf, Davidp, HappyCamper, Lightning jim, Sango123, A Man In Black, FlaBot, Xmoogle, Ground Zero, Wikidgood, Bgiltner, JdforresterBot, Q11, Harmil, NekoDaemon, Klosterdev, SportsMaster, RexNL, Gurch, Conwiki, Bennie Noakes, OrbitOne, Subversive, Diza, Amchow78, Lamrock, King of Hearts, Jersey Devil, Sherool, Jamesevanpilato, DVdm, Mmx1, Zimbabweed, The Rambling Man, Mahahahaneapneap, RussBot, ProphetPX, Bhny, Kilowattradio, Gaius Cornelius, Shaddack, Cryptic, NawlinWiki, Kibbitzer, Bachrach44, Badagnani, Jaxl, Robdurbar, Dputig07, Chal7ds, Davemck, Jcurious, Misza13, Pudist, Yano, Nut-meg, Sliggy, Allisonok, GeorgeC, Hixx, DeadEyeArrow, Schnob Reider, Kewp, David Nelson, Nlu, BarrettBrown, E tac, Nimmo, Anonimato, Paul Magnussen, Deville, Open2universe, Jules.LT, Schavira, Teiladnam, Theda, Arthur Rubin, Josh3580, Wsiegmund, GraemeL, Marco0009, Andjam, GoodSirJava, Johnl285, Draicone, Selmo, Kf4bdy, That Guy, From That Show!, Ja powa, A bit iffy, SmackBot, Alan Pascoe, Rosicrucian, Cdfreelancer, Cassandro, Bobet, InverseHypercube, KnowledgeOfSelf, McGeddon, Bjelleklang, Pgk, C.Fred, Clpo13, Verne Equinox, ProveIt, Kintetsubuffalo, Nil Einne, HalfShadow, Evanreyes, Aksi great, Gilliam, Portillo, Ohnoitsjamie, Nfgii, Cs-wolves, Martial Law, Amatulic, Chris the speller, Equiprimordial, Lord of the Left Hand, SlimJim, Jprg1966, BabuBhatt, Anchoress, Nemodomi, Moshe Constantine Hassan Al-Silverburg, Renamed user Sloane, Jerome Charles Potts, Canoro, Nedlum, Colonies Chris, Gracenotes, Stalepie, John Reaves, Deewhite, Gsp8181, Chendy, Lenin and McCarthy, Can't sleep, clown will eat me, MisterHand, LowVelocity, DHeyward, TheGerm, Brimba, OrphanBot, Onorem, Jwhites, Folksong, Morton devonshire, RedHillian, WikiTony, Chris71990, Badbilltucker, Bot0918, Simonapro, GavinOB, Dreadstar, Algore2008, Lcarscad, BullRangifer, Weregerbil, Kenscanna, Iridescence, DMacks, Wizardman, Xiutwel, Zoperd, Pilotguy, Coconuteire, Will Beback, Byelf2007, Cast, Ser Amantio di Nicolao, BrownHairedGirl, Kuru, John, Euchiasmus, Scientizzle, Heimstern, Bydand, Nolte, Ai565ai565, Tlesher, Arbustoo, Gilead, Michaelstor, Collect, IdeArchos, Shamrox, Countzer, Moth73, TFNorman, MarkH10, Danyak501, Meco, Waggers, Mets501, AdultSwim, Wvoutlaw2002, RG~enwiki, Psj333, Fluppy, Dr.K., Graball, Webucation, Freedom Fan, Quaeler, Dysprod1975, BranStark, Maddawg1967, Corykoski, Echofloripa, StuHarris, JoeBot, WikipediaBG, Cowicide, AlexLibman, EdRooney, JHP, Mrdthree, TobiasCunningham, Az1568, Anger22, Tawkerbot2, Mujinga, Magick93, Samnuva, Vistrix, Unidyne, Wikipediareader, CmdrObot, Tanthalas39, Baltech22, TheHerbalGerbil, Thewolfstar, LtWeesel, KnightLago, Kylu, Ckuzyk, Tim Long, Nakedtruth, Timtrent, Kitten b, Hopkapi, Azaadam88, HalJor, Cydebot, Nar Matteru, Wikien2009, Hydraton31, Treybien, Steel,

SyntaxError55, Meno25, Gogo Dodo, Kingclyde, Pascal.Tesson, The Real Jean-Luc, Arabhorse, Doug Weller, DumbBOT, Johnny Watson, RossyG, Omicronpersei8, Landroo, Gimmetrow, Tortillovsky, Inoculatedcities, The eagle, VectorCell, Thijs!bot, Epbr123, Qwyrxian, Schicksal, Serpent-A, PerfectStorm, Gobuffs10, Mojo Hand, Möchtegern, John254, CameoAppearance, Mokkan88, EdJohnston, CharlotteWebb, Tocino, Tree Hugger, Dawnseeker2000, Natalie Erin, Eleuther, RED DAVE, Hackstar18, Mezlo, John Smythe, Cyclonenim, Vafthrudnir, AntiVandalBot, Gpaulos, Yuval Y, Widefox, Rambone, FrasierC, Seaphoto, Tangerines, Milesflint, Smartse, Postlewaight, Wikiscaper, Dylan Lake, Yellowdesk, Vulcanhacker, Crispyfritters, Dgexodus, Leuko, Freepsbane, Ninten, Barek, Nathanalex, Inks.LWC, Ericoides, Janejellyroll, 90rock, John Ryan, Yugigx60, Hut 8.5, GurchBot, Smith Jones, MrRandomGuy, TAnthony, Drdak, Kerotan, .anacondabot, Meeples, Pablothegreat85, Magioladitis, Jay942942, VoABot II, AuburnPilot, Pilgriminal, Yandman, Kinston eagle, Richrobison, Gabe1972, Farqis, Roguestate, WODUP, Frater volen, Not a dog, Umeboshi, Sgr927, Zombiema7, Schumi555, JAltman752, Ivangeotsky, Glen, Ninja Jordan, DerHexer, Edward321, Rebel lonedog, Valerius Tygart, Skylights76, Dyst, AlgulSiento, DGG, Oroso, Gwern, Tracer9999, Nathanmcginty, Stephenchou0722, MartinBot, Grandia01, Tvoz, BiggunSid, Zilax, R'n'B, CommonsDelinker, Brothejr, PrestonH, DanJ, Yrgh, VivaRiva, Grazia11, J.delanoy, Perry Logan, Trusilver, Tikiwont, Uncle Dick, Truthunmasked, Joe Burd, FMAanime, Pikaraichu, Ian.thomson, PC78, Testrundelta, Darth Mike, VeritasInTheUK, TomCat4680, Roslagen, Davidrossjones, Shawn in Montreal, Athene cunicularia, Fairness And Accuracy For All, Aboutmovies, Zero Serenity, JayJasper, Chriswiki, Noahcs, AntiSpamBot, Tustiman, FRYGUY6887, Khalid red, Gareth0105, DadaNeem, SJP, Gredsen, Thirty3na3rd, DH85868993, Gwen Gale, Mike V, Redrocket, Qlj, Codecsubzero, Scott Illini, Andy Marchbanks, Useight, Tirk, Duchamps comb, Thebearwillriseagain, Sam Blacketer, Tony Darkgrave, VolkovBot, Melkiresha, Jeff G., MackDieselX27, I'mDown, Katydidit, WOSlinker, Philip Trueman, Taketheveilcerpintaxt, Hmjgriffon, Martinevans123, Stacks77, Oshwah, Cosmic Latte, Pwnage8, Thycid, Dchall1, Steven J. Anderson, Lradrama, Rbpolsen, AllGloryToTheHypnotoad, LeaveSleaves, Hamitr, Ephix, Dj rizla, Cremepuff222, Steve Checkoway, Wikiisawesome, Harpakhrad11, Quindraco, Witchzilla, Nikolai Revolutionary, Kurowoofwoof111, Ezra2000, Billinghurst, Enigmaman, Benchilada, Serious Cat, Tritoneking, Hereward77, Unclebif4, Bjornyvan, RaseaC, Justmeherenow, The Devil's Advocate, Edkollin, Dstarsfan06, Dick Shane, Quantpole, Jimmi Hugh, Krautukie, Malskl2, Daveh4h, Mk05406, Theoneintraining, Cosprings, Lightbreather, Mac87, Spartan, Ostap R, Electrostatic1, JDoesmith, Vexorg, Dawn Bard, Alex Middleton, Fesco, Trigaranus, Patlovesmj, Triwbe, Manchurian, Ccosborn, Gavinthorp, Dala0, Digwuren, RucasHost, Happysailor, Flyer22, Joebonscott, Arbor to SJ, Ventur, Adrock87, Monegasque, Thirdpartycontroller, The Slowphase, Plastic0, Brokendata, Nuttycoconut, Lightmouse, Shink X, Bushdid911, Fratrep, Nancy, Svick, Dravecky, Maelgwnbot, Videmus Omnia, Dabomb87, Asuf938rhfn, Escape Orbit, Stillwaterising, Tomdobb, Niall Flanagan, Raneksi, Martarius, Elassint, ClueBot, Xfearbefore, Daffydavid, Tomsaveus, Dankitman, Joehoe665, Edi43, Facistfuq, Binksternet, Hutcher, Palmerklees, Snigbrook, Djdetroit, The Thing That Should Not Be, All Hallow's Wraith, Plastikspork, Ninbit, Eduction, MaxBishop, EAEB, ChesterCharge, Thalkyudes, Ericstrategy, Skeeboo, Jimmyledbyvoices, PetemcCool, Tobey2, Robby.is.on, Camdoon, LeighMet, Jld123, Niceguyedc, Oddibe, Roflcopter126, Kinlaso, Counteraction, MantisEars, Byates5637, John Nevard, Niteshift36, Mindstalk, Markshark4, NuclearWarfare, Geaslaha, TheRedPenOfDoom, El Juche, WOLFSERPENTCROWRAT, Byebye6121, Pickaname, ChrisHamburg, Mlaffs, Calor, Joe83420, Thingg, Gogogolf, Kristallion9966, Scalhotrod, Muhammad Cthulhu, OddibeKerfeld, PCHS-NJROTC, Katanada, MelonBot, Conspiracy Smasher, Dannyoak, Rothchild, Apparition11, SF007, Plasmadyn, DumZiBoT, Doenitz~enwiki, XLinkBot, Timbermile99, Fastily, AnotherSolipsist, Gnowor, Burningview, Mcfrandy, Nomoskedasticity, Imunuri, Dthomsen8, Skarebo, Cmr08, HarlandQPitt, Mr cutty, Dubmill, Good Olfactory, Airplaneman, Thatguyflint, Kbdankbot, HexaChord, CalumH93, Addbot, JBsupreme, Monkey Sides, Willking1979, Ismokeherbs, Grandscribe, Lefick, Ronhjones, Dirtylemons, Bibblybobbbob, Vishnava, Noozgroop, Swahrheit, Jpoelma13, Cst17, Download, Unowen7, FTF85, Bigcock0, Mshith, Buster7, Glane23, Akwilks, Emojojo2002, Favonian, Kyle1278, Evadinggrid, Democracy to information, Loose Brains, Hcuk, Tassedethe, Tokyogaijin, Dayewalker, Tide rolls, Femcamper, Verbal, Lightbot, OlEnglish, Abduallah mohammed, Film Music Lover, Rodericksilly, Blah28948, Luckas-bot, Wtc7waspulled, Yobot, Worldbruce, WikiDan61, JJARichardson, Tohd8BohaithuGh1, Ptbotgourou, DJBobHoskinsGoingMentalInADustbin, Kresk, Mrstooge, Bugnot, Zombie1334, Brougham96, Noiselull, Happy Funtime, Criticalthoughtya, The7thdr, Lolipod, Bbb23, AnomieBOT, Robertcan, Jim1138, IRP, ItsAlwaysLupus, JackieBot, Piano non troppo, Mec1969nc, IrFactor, Flewis, Mahmudmasri, Materialscientist, Citation bot, GB fan, ArthurBot, Quebec99, Kalumba, Xqbot, BlueGumHunter, Capricorn42, TracyMcClark, Renaissancee, Blitz77, Gilo1969, Arbalest Mike, Dradeb1, Sefor4, Ub0r, Call me Bubba, ArkinAardvark, SLCMemento, INeverCry, Doulos Christos, A Quest For Knowledge, GhalyBot, Dodder0, Junsun, Shadowjams, Erik9, VasOling, RicoRichmond, Lionelt, Calibrador, Tiramisoo, Adam9389, BimboBaggins, GodivaCake, Bocher, Rudolph Davis, Skibereen, KuroiShiroi, BillyJack193, Kodylikessushi, Haeinous, Markeilz, XcoolmanX, Animus999, 44superguy44, Helajuvanut134, Jevulmikel134, Jinniuop, Justicelovespeace, Cs32en, Illuminatidvds, Hallonius, PigFlu Oink, Blargh29, Gaba p, I dream of horses, WikiAntPedia, Pheneviox, Homedog66, Supreme Deliciousness, Skyerise, Thewatchdog2012, Fat&Happy, Thx11384ebsin, Gingermint, Atulananda, Freedomforus, Just4lulz, SoFDMC, Mmmbrownn, SW3 5DL, Nategray79, I AM OmniCore, Wikiwikiwawawowo, Nimish Gautam, FoxBot, Serpentdove, Hoshide, Patriot911, Mardana, Varks Spira, DA1, Diannaa, Usability 2, TexianPolitico, Iceman247, Tbhotch, Fruitcakeweather, TheMesquito, Minimac, Wikistk, Dj6ual, RjwilmsiBot, Bento00, Alph Bot, ButOnMethItIs, Slaja, DASHBot, Dartuxmask, EmausBot, Iceman1777, And we drown, Atwarwiththem, Desertroad, Tayyeb Jaan, Yuilen, R3ll3k, RenamedUser01302013, Ing. Garin, Cking15, Sentient Planet, Winner 42, InfoWarrior77777777x8, Whmagill, K6ka, Mojokabobo, John Shandy`, Ronk01, ZéroBot, Empeda, Justinthetwit, Sgerbic, Cobaltcigs, Vyeh, MH1987, Mdmday, Ariesk47, L Kensington, Shrigley, Mentibot, Wisdomtenacityfocus, ThePowerofX, Terraflorin, Kuttaps, TYelliot, Naiadea, DemonicPartyHat, Jalal Hasan JH, LM2000, ClueBot NG, Mansmokingacigar, Notanipokay, Sugarcube73, Wikilearner1980, Somedifferentstuff, MelbourneStar, This lousy T-shirt, Daeditfiend, Kruger1191~enwiki, BakuninGoldmanKropotkin, GLPer4truth, Esotericcode, Cybermann, GuitarWizard90, Widr, Delaywaves, RoadHouse, JordoCo, Cyrrk, Anupmehra, Wizikj, Parksand, Kinaro, Tom-1674, BG19bot, Jmwikiacc, Neptune's Trident, Karinsa, Juro2351, DPBT1, Zach Vega, Versace1608, Altaïr, Dhf510, The Almightey Drill, Harizotoh9, Wikilov3r1982, Squirelewis, Shaun, Lommaren, VivaWikipedia, BattyBot, Jeremy112233, Arr4, Cyberbot II, Myxomatosis57, YFdyh-bot, FoCuSandLeArN, Cwobeel, Reverend Mick man34, Charles Essie, CrackaSteve, Lugia2453, MattSucci, StillStanding-247, ExclusiveAgent, Asaust, NormShields, Infowarriorusmc, Malerooster, Michaelt54, Clairmccascall, Blaue Max, Epicgenius, CsDix, Skylights75, MrJohnFranson, Wudusa, Offspringholy, Repoman98, LanthanumK, Michipedian, Headcornyou, Alfy32, Everymorning, Felt friend, Rossbawse, EvergreenFir, Backendgaming, ElHef, Whatdidyousayni99a, Beerest355, KurtWags3, Steeletrap, Thevideodrome, Ugog Nizdast, LahmacunKebab, Gretchen Mädelnick, MrScorch6200, Renren8123, Stamptrader, JaconaFrere, Retartist, Meowcatzmeow, ReformedBeliever, MirandaKeurr, ConcordeMandalorian, RustinHamster, WikiEditor69BigNuts, Zumoarirodoka, Rogerroyal, Filedelinkerbot, P-123, SantiLak, Malomajic, Owais Khursheed, Hahawinmofo, Brother Samson, Seemslegitbrah, A guy saved by Jesus, Libertarian12111971, Aido46, The Last Arietta, CODY TRUTH, Fixit12345, LesVegas, LincolnWars, Flaperdoodle, DrGONOB, EllenSaturn, Vinnypizzalover, Colef150, Syntheticrebellion, BristolianHD, Rollondeodorant, Squinge, SmithBama, Jfifer256, J A GRANDA, Zornbratton, KasparBot, Infoforall11, Prestondtenglish, PaulBustion88, Salamanca1981, JJMC89, Volkstod, KSFT, NeuronMaster, TheFanatical, Drone121, NerdPriest, The Independent 100, Extraknutch2342, The Independent 1981 and Anonymous: 1254

- **Belizean Grove** *Source:* https://en.wikipedia.org/wiki/Belizean_Grove?oldid=611370780 *Contributors:* JeffHos, TheRingess, Wasted Time R, Anomalocaris, SMcCandlish, Binksternet, Solar-Wind, AgnosticPreachersKid, Yobot, FrescoBot, Loutime, MathirJayanadine, RjwilmsiBot, DASHBot, Delcydrew, RobertBDurham and Anonymous: 6

- **Elizabeth Crocker Bowers** *Source:* https://en.wikipedia.org/wiki/Elizabeth_Crocker_Bowers?oldid=664584405 *Contributors:* Koavf, Superslum, SmackBot, GoodDay, Bejnar, Will Beback, BrownHairedGirl, Cydebot, Waacstats, Here2fixCategorizations, Johnpacklambert, Koplimek, Aboutmovies, Aciram, BOTijo, Binksternet, TypoBoy, Brewcrewer, Jeanenawhitney, SchreiberBike, RogDel, Lightbot, Yobot, Bob Burkhardt, Jesse V., RjwilmsiBot, Cjeffery.geo and Anonymous: 5

- **George Sterling** *Source:* https://en.wikipedia.org/wiki/George_Sterling?oldid=675627560 *Contributors:* Liftarn, Charles Matthews, Dagon~enwiki, Dpbsmith, Cxarli, D6, Andrew Norman, EdgeOfEternity, Woohookitty, Rjwilmsi, Koavf, Emiellaiendiay, Howcheng, PhilipC, WamBamBoozle, SmackBot, KnowledgeOfSelf, Ohnoitsjamie, Bluebot, Kasyapa, PoetryForEveryone, Ser Amantio di Nicolao, Dicklyon, Tmangray, Stargzer, Donswaim, Keraunos, Midnightdreary, Waacstats, Aboutmovies, GrahamHardy, Mike Cline, Mercurywoodrose, Martin451, Tomaxer, Polbot, ELCore, Dannyl58, Seaaron, Binksternet, Fyyer, XLinkBot, Lexaxis7, Good Olfactory, DOI bot, Tassedethe, Pernoctus, Yobot, Vinceemery, Green Cardamom, CA Legacy, Lotje, Arcadia616, RjwilmsiBot, The Stick Man, Helpful Pixie Bot, BG19bot, VIAFbot, Monkbot, KasparBot and Anonymous: 21

- **Haig Patigian** *Source:* https://en.wikipedia.org/wiki/Haig_Patigian?oldid=674768846 *Contributors:* Neutrality, Carptrash, Mandarax, Koavf, Lockley, Whyaduck, Threeafterthree, TA-ME, Ser Amantio di Nicolao, Cydebot, Barticus88, Dsp13, Waacstats, EtienneDolet, Johnpacklambert, Aboutmovies, M-le-mot-dit, WRK, Binksternet, Andranikpasha, Solar-Wind, Another Believer, Addbot, Bunnyhop11, FriscoKnight, Hovhannesk, RjwilmsiBot, TjBot, Helpful Pixie Bot, Yerevantsi, ChrisGualtieri, KasparBot and Anonymous: 3

- **Ina Coolbrith** *Source:* https://en.wikipedia.org/wiki/Ina_Coolbrith?oldid=677340307 *Contributors:* Vicki Rosenzweig, Lquilter, Dpbsmith, Cxarli, Braaropolis, Gamaliel, Kate, D6, Xezbeth, Bender235, Philip Cross, Logologist, Scott5114, Stemonitis, Woohookitty, Sesmith, BD2412, Koavf, Rogerd, Vegaswikian, Wavelength, Yllosubmarine, Nogood, Howcheng, BorgQueen, SmackBot, Elonka, Nihonjoe, Gilliam, PrimeHunter, Sadads, Ser Amantio di Nicolao, Joseph Solis in Australia, Catherineyronwode, Billy Hathorn, Cydebot, MainlyTwelve, Steven.Harris, ARTEST4ECHO, Porlob, NE2, BoatMesa, Ling.Nut, Johnpacklambert, HarZim, Aboutmovies, Scewing, Mercurywoodrose, Thmazing, Woilorio, SQL, Mountnebo, Rosiestep, Seaaron, Finetooth, Binksternet, Dagosti, P. S. Burton, Sun Creator, DumZiBoT, Good Olfactory, Addbot, Malconfort, Lightbot, Yobot, Samson22911, Phelps1362, Alialiac, Green Cardamom, M2545, OgreBot, FriscoKnight, CA Legacy, Arcadia616, Look2See1, KHearts, ZéroBot, H3llBot, Sonnemon, 11 Arlington, RayneVanDunem, Helpful Pixie Bot, Michael Barera, VIAFbot, Xenxax, Monkbot, KasparBot and Anonymous: 12

- **James F. Bowman** *Source:* https://en.wikipedia.org/wiki/James_F._Bowman?oldid=657265623 *Contributors:* Maurreen, Rjwilmsi, Koavf, BorgQueen, SmackBot, Ser Amantio di Nicolao, Cydebot, Melos Antropon, Waacstats, Aboutmovies, Rosiestep, Scottyoak2, Binksternet, Darx9url, Ulric1313, RjwilmsiBot and Helpful Pixie Bot

- **John of Nepomuk** *Source:* https://en.wikipedia.org/wiki/John_of_Nepomuk?oldid=685969756 *Contributors:* AxelBoldt, Vargenau, Wetman, Qertis, Mirv, Halibutt, Guy Peters, Matt Borak, Matthead, Formeruser-81, Piotrus, Känsterle~enwiki, Mikko Paananen, Klemen Kocjancic, DanielCD, AlanBarrett, Jnestorius, Ludger1961, Man vyi, Polylerus, JohnAlbertRigali, Kusma, Ghirlandajo, Hailey C. Shannon, Julo, Cuchullain, Dpr, Rjwilmsi, Titoxd, Janothird, YurikBot, Briaboru, Hede2000, Eleassar, GeeJo, Snek01, Bota47, AjaxSmack, Sotakeit, Rms125a@hotmail.com, Abune, Diligent, Criticality, SmackBot, Reedy, Yopie, Srnec, Hmains, Ludi, Lamadude, MalafayaBot, Mathiasrex, Epiphyllumlover, Iridescent, Angeldeb82, CmdrObot, 5-HT8, Vaquero100, Cavalcabo, Cydebot, Jackyd101, Thijs!bot, Wikid77, Mojo Hand, Top.Squark, Nick Number, Fayenatic london, JAnDbot, Waacstats, STBot, CommonsDelinker, Tulkolahten, TomS TDotO, BrokenSphere, LordAnubisBOT, M-le-mot-dit, Pinea, Idioma-bot, VolkovBot, Dickstracke, Ar-wiki, Markhalpern, SieBot, BotMultichill, Calabraxthis, Joe Gatt, Vanished user ewfisn2348tui2f8n2fio2utjfeoi210r39jf, ClueBot, TIY, Wkharrisjr, BurgererSF~enwiki, EstherLois, RogDel, Vegas949, MystBot, Addbot, Lightbot, Luckas-bot, Yobot, Ptbotgourou, Rdancer, Roltz, Renessaince, Mike Hayes, Bob Burkhardt, Immaculateperfection, Xqbot, RibotBOT, Steindy, FrescoBot, Cannolis, RedBot, Lotje, Ridiculus mus, Ato 01, EmausBot, Djembayz, ZéroBot, PBS-AWB, The Nut, Cimmerian praetor, Naryd, Scythia, ClueBot NG, Urharec, Gerald Spitzner, Blanicky, Andyman06, Tiggyt, Lfdder, Бучач-Львів, SuDomek, Realcatholic15, Silasspat, PeregrinuxXX and Anonymous: 51

- **Philip Weiss** *Source:* https://en.wikipedia.org/wiki/Philip_Weiss?oldid=678533558 *Contributors:* Ashley Y, Bobo192, SCEhardt, BD2412, Koavf, Jweiss11, Atrix20, RussBot, Deodar~enwiki, BomBom, Crystallina, Classicfilms, Bluebot, Ronsard, Colonies Chris, Mokeyboy, Doug Bell, Joseph Solis in Australia, CmdrObot, Anthony Bradbury, Cydebot, DumbBOT, Nishidani, G-Dett, Carolmooredc, NSH001, Cjs2111, Ruthfulbarbarity, Henrylievsay, Telecineguy, Proscript, Gr8opinionater, Lucretius99, Paladin R.T., BOTarate, John Bahrain, Addbot, Yobot, ThaddeusB, Jim1138, AMuseo, Srich32977, LivingBot, DareToBeJackRoss, Plot Spoiler, Full-date unlinking bot, Reaper Eternal, WillNess, RjwilmsiBot, Saharawiki, John Cline, I.Casaubon, Widr, Helpful Pixie Bot, BG19bot, BattyBot, Dlv999, ChrisGualtieri, Decathlete, Webclient101, VIAFbot, Malerooster, InfoDataMonger, KasparBot and Anonymous: 37

- **Richard McCaslin** *Source:* https://en.wikipedia.org/wiki/Richard_McCaslin?oldid=655508514 *Contributors:* Bearcat, Fschoenm, Mandarax, Ground Zero, SmackBot, Robofish, George100, Waacstats, Emeraude, Trusilver, Addbot, Lucasperkins, AnomieBOT, Erik9bot, Wgolf, ChrisGualtieri, WordSeventeen and Anonymous: 8

- **Sara Jane Lippincott** *Source:* https://en.wikipedia.org/wiki/Sara_Jane_Lippincott?oldid=677249787 *Contributors:* Magnus Manske, Wetman, Orlady, Wayward, BD2412, Koavf, Ground Zero, Bhoeble, Lar, TooPotato, SmackBot, Hmains, Rudowsky, Ser Amantio di Nicolao, John, Myopic Bookworm, Amalas, PKT, JamesAM, Midnightdreary, Waacstats, Nyttend, Johnpacklambert, Scewing, Josette, Oculi, Maralia, Binksternet, Jeanenawhitney, Debresser, Yobot, LilHelpa, Green Cardamom, Haeinous, Full-date unlinking bot, RjwilmsiBot, John of Reading, Khazar2, VIAFbot, Watermonki, Mediavalia, KasparBot and Anonymous: 11

- **Significant Others (novel)** *Source:* https://en.wikipedia.org/wiki/Significant_Others_(novel)?oldid=649790010 *Contributors:* Bearcat, Grutness, Personman, Dialectric, Cydebot, Aristophanes68, TAnthony, Clavecin, Oaklandgayasian, Sgeureka, GrahamHardy, Henry Merrivale, Good Olfactory, Lightbot, Yobot, AnomieBOT, LilHelpa, Wikignome0529, VioletSeraphim, Helpful Pixie Bot, BattyBot and Anonymous: 3

- **The Family (club)** *Source:* https://en.wikipedia.org/wiki/The_Family_(club)?oldid=684398704 *Contributors:* Bumm13, TheRingess, Vegaswikian, President Rhapsody, A Doon, Hmains, Miranker, Cydebot, The Anomebot2, DadaNeem, GrahamHardy, Mercurywoodrose, Rontrigger, Oculi, Binksternet, Plastikspork, Tvalleau, Trivialist, Vansud, Blethering Scot, Yobot, AnomieBOT, JacklynD, Vinceemery, FriscoKnight,

BuddhasFingers, Torro de la Pinta, Philafrenzy, A wild Rattata, Amyziteng, Ginfizz, Helpful Pixie Bot, Strike Eagle, Clubwiki, !996AAA, Swenssonjohn, Monkbot and Anonymous: 11

- **The Secret Rulers of the World** *Source:* https://en.wikipedia.org/wiki/The_Secret_Rulers_of_the_World?oldid=681064393 *Contributors:* Emperor, Tom harrison, Ashley Pomeroy, Kyven, Marudubshinki, Semi-awesome, Dadu~enwiki, RussBot, GeorgeC, Bishop^, Pegship, Tower~enwiki, SmackBot, Master Deusoma, Zleitzen, Blueboar, Byelf2007, Lambiam, JzG, N1h1l, Naaman Brown, Dl2000, Hu12, Ale_jrb, GHe, Cydebot, Trasel, Doug Weller, Floridasand, J'onn J'onzz, KConWiki, Shawn in Montreal, Noahcs, FuegoFish, Aeqea, Wikiuserphil, Insanity Incarnate, Proscript, Binksternet, Trivialist, PseudoOne, Greek2, Grayfell, Spartamo, Jessi1989, Anthony of the Desert, Lothar von Richthofen, Visite fortuitement prolongée, ClueBot NG, Northamerica1000 and Anonymous: 34

3.2 Images

- **File:005-a-Ruby-kindles-in-the-vine-810x1146.jpg** *Source:* https://upload.wikimedia.org/wikipedia/commons/0/08/ 005-a-Ruby-kindles-in-the-vine-810x1146.jpg *License:* Public domain *Contributors:* *The Rubaiyat of Omar Khayyam* (1905, 1912)[1] *Original artist:* Adelaide Hanscom

- **File:1907_Cremation_of_Care.jpg** *Source:* https://upload.wikimedia.org/wikipedia/commons/9/94/1907_Cremation_of_Care.jpg *License:* Public domain *Contributors:* http://books.google.com/books?id=KTBIAAAAIAAJ *The Bohemian Jinks: A Treatise* (1908)], page 94. *Original artist:* Gabriel Moulin

- **File:1909_Grove_Play_dress_rehearsal.jpg** *Source:* https://upload.wikimedia.org/wikipedia/commons/6/6a/1909_Grove_Play_dress_ rehearsal.jpg *License:* Public domain *Contributors:* http://www.archive.org/details/groveplaysofbohe02boherich *Original artist:* ?

- **File:Abierce.jpg** *Source:* https://upload.wikimedia.org/wikipedia/commons/5/57/Abierce.jpg *License:* Public domain *Contributors:* http://etext.lib.virginia.edu/eaf/authors/ab.htm#Other, EAF Author: Ambrose Bierce Collection, Clifton Waller Barrett Library of American Literature, Special Collections, University of Virginia Library.
  Original artist: ?

- **File:AlexJonesWithFans.jpg** *Source:* https://upload.wikimedia.org/wikipedia/commons/f/f9/AlexJonesWithFans.jpg *License:* CC BY 2.0 *Contributors:* http://www.flickr.com/photos/72476440@N00/177453065/ *Original artist:* Nick Mollberg

- **File:Alex_Jones_NY.jpg** *Source:* https://upload.wikimedia.org/wikipedia/commons/4/41/Alex_Jones_NY.jpg *License:* CC BY 2.0 *Contributors:* http://www.flickr.com/photos/14638975@N04/2220050399/ *Original artist:* 911conspiracy

- **File:Ambox_current_red.svg** *Source:* https://upload.wikimedia.org/wikipedia/commons/9/98/Ambox_current_red.svg *License:* CC0 *Contributors:* self-made, inspired by Gnome globe current event.svg, using Information icon3.svg and Earth clip art.svg *Original artist:* Vipersnake151, penubag, Tkgd2007 (clock)

- **File:Belizean_Grove_banner.gif** *Source:* https://upload.wikimedia.org/wikipedia/en/8/86/Belizean_Grove_banner.gif *License:* Fair use *Contributors:*
  belizeangrove.com *Original artist:* ?

- **File:BohemianClubOwl1.jpg** *Source:* https://upload.wikimedia.org/wikipedia/commons/4/42/BohemianClubOwl1.jpg *License:* Public domain *Contributors:* Own work (Original text: *I created this work entirely by myself.*) *Original artist:* Binksternet (talk)

- **File:Bohemian_Club,_San_Francisco.jpg** *Source:* https://upload.wikimedia.org/wikipedia/commons/2/22/Bohemian_Club%2C_San_ Francisco.jpg *License:* CC BY-SA 4.0 *Contributors:* Own work *Original artist:* Wikophile1

- **File:Bohemian_Grove_Camp_-_Garnett,_Sterling,_London.jpg** *Source:* https://upload.wikimedia.org/wikipedia/commons/4/4c/ Bohemian_Grove_Camp_-_Garnett%2C_Sterling%2C_London.jpg *License:* Public domain *Contributors:* http://www.archive.org/stream/ pacificmonthly00woodrich#page/n49/mode/1up *Original artist:* Binksternet

- **File:Books-aj.svg_aj_ashton_01b.svg** *Source:* https://upload.wikimedia.org/wikipedia/commons/2/29/Books-aj.svg_aj_ashton_01b.svg *License:* Public domain *Contributors:* Self-made. Just switched the color of the books. Similar to Image:Books-aj.svg aj ashton 01c.png by Pegship. *Original artist:* Rocket000

- **File:Bret_Harte_Memorial_A.jpg** *Source:* https://upload.wikimedia.org/wikipedia/commons/a/ac/Bret_Harte_Memorial_A.jpg *License:* Public domain *Contributors:* http://siris-artinventories.si.edu/ipac20/ipac.jsp?&profile=all&source=~{}!siartinventories&uri=full= 3100001~{}!318520~{}!0#focus *Original artist:* Jo Mora

- **File:Commons-logo.svg** *Source:* https://upload.wikimedia.org/wikipedia/en/4/4a/Commons-logo.svg *License:* ? *Contributors:* ? *Original artist:* ?

- **File:Coolbrith_headstone.jpg** *Source:* https://upload.wikimedia.org/wikipedia/commons/9/91/Coolbrith_headstone.jpg *License:* CC BY-SA 3.0 *Contributors:* Own work *Original artist:* Binksternet

- **File:Czechowicz_St._John_Nepomuk.jpg** *Source:* https://upload.wikimedia.org/wikipedia/commons/5/55/Czechowicz_St._John_ Nepomuk.jpg *License:* Public domain *Contributors:* www.pinakoteka.zascianek.pl *Original artist:* Szymon Czechowicz

- **File:Gay_flag.svg** *Source:* https://upload.wikimedia.org/wikipedia/commons/6/68/Gay_flag.svg *License:* Public domain *Contributors:* SVG source (version of 17:56, 30 Sep 2011): *Original artist:* Guanaco and subsequent editors

- **File:GeorgeSterling.JPG** *Source:* https://upload.wikimedia.org/wikipedia/commons/8/89/GeorgeSterling.JPG *License:* Public domain *Contributors:* Extracted from public domain PDF version of *Overland Monthly*, December 1927 *Original artist:* Mike Cline

- **File:George_Sterling_with_art_1907.jpg** *Source:* https://upload.wikimedia.org/wikipedia/commons/1/16/George_Sterling_with_art_1907. jpg *License:* Public domain *Contributors:* http://content.cdlib.org/ark:/13030/tf9m3nb7b2/?layout=metadata&brand=calisphere *Original artist:* Unknown

- **File:Little_Pilgrim_Masthead1855.jpg** *Source:* https://upload.wikimedia.org/wikipedia/commons/e/eb/Little_Pilgrim_Masthead1855.jpg *License:* Public domain *Contributors:* American children's periodicals, 1789 - 1872: [1] *Original artist:* 1854 sketch by Mr. Darley (information found on the source page) Uploaded by User:Epousesquecido (also w:User: Epousesquecido)

- **File:Maynard_Dixon_-_The_Apparition_of_Cuchulainn.jpg** *Source:* https://upload.wikimedia.org/wikipedia/commons/b/be/ Maynard_Dixon_-_The_Apparition_of_Cuchulainn.jpg *License:* Public domain *Contributors:* http://www.archive.org/details/ groveplaysofbohe02boherich *Original artist:* Maynard Dixon

- **File:Owl_Shrine.jpg** *Source:* https://upload.wikimedia.org/wikipedia/commons/8/8e/Owl_Shrine.jpg *License:* CC BY-SA 3.0 *Contributors:* Own work *Original artist:* Aarkwilde

- **File:P_vip.svg** *Source:* https://upload.wikimedia.org/wikipedia/en/6/69/P_vip.svg *License:* PD *Contributors:* ? *Original artist:* ?

- **File:Pflueger-MetLife-Patigian.jpg** *Source:* https://upload.wikimedia.org/wikipedia/commons/6/6b/Pflueger-MetLife-Patigian.jpg *License:* Public domain *Contributors:* Own work *Original artist:* Binksternet

- **File:Question_book-new.svg** *Source:* https://upload.wikimedia.org/wikipedia/en/9/99/Question_book-new.svg *License:* Cc-by-sa-3.0 *Contributors:*
  Created from scratch in Adobe Illustrator. Based on Image:Question book.png created by User:Equazcion *Original artist:* Tkgd2007

- **File:Quill_and_ink.svg** *Source:* https://upload.wikimedia.org/wikipedia/commons/c/c4/Quill_and_ink.svg *License:* CC BY-SA 2.5 *Contributors:* Own work *Original artist:* Ebrenc at Catalan Wikipedia

- **File:Radio_icon.png** *Source:* https://upload.wikimedia.org/wikipedia/commons/1/1d/Radio_icon.png *License:* Public domain *Contributors:* ? *Original artist:* ?

- **File:SF_From_Marin_Highlands3.jpg** *Source:* https://upload.wikimedia.org/wikipedia/commons/d/da/SF_From_Marin_Highlands3.jpg *License:* Public domain *Contributors:* en:User:Paul.h *Original artist:* en:User:Paul.h

- **File:Sara_jane_Lippincott_ca1850.jpg** *Source:* https://upload.wikimedia.org/wikipedia/commons/8/80/Sara_jane_Lippincott_ca1850.jpg *License:* Public domain *Contributors:*
  Original artist: Southworth & Hawes

- **File:Sketch_of_Bohemian_Grove_Main_Stage_by_Porter_Garnett.jpg** *Source:* https://upload.wikimedia.org/wikipedia/commons/ f/f6/Sketch_of_Bohemian_Grove_Main_Stage_by_Porter_Garnett.jpg *License:* Public domain *Contributors:* <a data-x-rel='nofollow' class='external text' href='http://books.google.com/books?id=QeEsAAAAYAAJ'>*The Green Knight: A Vision*</a>, 1911 Grove Play *Original artist:* Porter Garnett

- **File:Songs_from_the_Golden_Gate.jpg** *Source:* https://upload.wikimedia.org/wikipedia/commons/b/b5/Songs_from_the_Golden_Gate.jpg *License:* Public domain *Contributors:* http://www.dsloan.com/Auctions/A12/Coolbrithcover.jpg *Original artist:* Coolbrith

- **File:Speaker_Icon.svg** *Source:* https://upload.wikimedia.org/wikipedia/commons/2/21/Speaker_Icon.svg *License:* Public domain *Contributors:* ? *Original artist:* ?

- **File:St._Ian_Nepomuk._Buchach_3.jpg** *Source:* https://upload.wikimedia.org/wikipedia/commons/2/29/St._Ian_Nepomuk._Buchach_3. jpg *License:* CC BY-SA 3.0 *Contributors:* Own work *Original artist:* Бучач-Львів

- **File:Text_document_with_red_question_mark.svg** *Source:* https://upload.wikimedia.org/wikipedia/commons/a/a4/Text_document_with_ red_question_mark.svg *License:* Public domain *Contributors:* Created by bdesham with Inkscape; based upon Text-x-generic.svg from the Tango project. *Original artist:* Benjamin D. Esham (bdesham)

- **File:The_Family_club_entrance_door.jpg** *Source:* https://upload.wikimedia.org/wikipedia/commons/f/fd/The_Family_club_entrance_ door.jpg *License:* Public domain *Contributors:* Own work *Original artist:* Binksternet

- **File:Wroclaw_OstrowTunski-swJanNepomucen.jpg** *Source:* https://upload.wikimedia.org/wikipedia/commons/a/a4/Wroclaw_ OstrowTunski-swJanNepomucen.jpg *License:* Public domain *Contributors:* No machine-readable source provided. Own work assumed (based on copyright claims). *Original artist:* No machine-readable author provided. Julo assumed (based on copyright claims).

- **File:Y24-Wtc-september-5.jpg** *Source:* https://upload.wikimedia.org/wikipedia/commons/a/af/Y24-Wtc-september-5.jpg *License:* CC BY 2.0 *Contributors:* http://www.flickr.com/photos/jul/104836555/in/set-72057594070873683/ *Original artist:* Julien Menichini

3.3 Content license